JEREMY PANG'S

JEREMY PANG'S

SCHOOL OF

WOK

DELICIOUS ASIAN FOOD IN MINUTES

hamlyn

To my dearest kids, tiny little Rosa, who turned up in the world the month
I started writing this book, and to her thoughtful and loving big brother
Theo – the kindest mini wok star I have ever met.

First published in Great Britain in 2022 by Hamlyn,
a division of Octopus Publishing Group Ltd,
Carmelite House, 50 Victoria Embankment,
London EC4Y 0DZ
www.octopusbooks.co.uk
www.octopusbooksusa.com

An Hachette UK Company
www.hachette.co.uk

Distributed in the US by Hachette Book Group, 1290 Avenue of the Americas,
4th and 5th Floors, New York, NY 10104

Distributed in Canada by Canadian Manda Group, 664 Annette St., Toronto,
Ontario, Canada M6S 2C8

978-0-60063-730-1

A CIP catalogue record for this book is available from the British Library.

Printed and bound in China.

10 9 8 7 6 5 4 3 2 1

Publisher: Eleanor Maxfield
Senior Editor: Pauline Bache
Art Director: Jonathan Christie
Copy Editor: Jo Smith
Design: Smith & Gilmour
Illustration: Freya Deabill
Photographer: Kris Kirkham
Food Stylist: Rosie Reynolds
Props Stylist: Morag Farquhar
Senior Production Manager: Allison Gonsalves

CONTENTS

LEARN LAUGH EAT

This book is a celebration of all the victories, big or small, that the School of Wok family – past, present and future – has achieved. School of Wok is our little Asian cookery school, set in Covent Garden, London, which has blossomed and grown over the years as we've shared it with hundreds of thousands of eager learners (and eaters!). You may have come across our online video tutorials, fun foodie inventions or cookware, but not yet had the chance to visit us at the school. So, this very first School of Wok cookery book offers a selection of recipes to help you start your School of Wok journey in your own kitchen.

If you do get a chance to visit, our school is the heart and soul of where the magic happens. It's the hub for our team to meet, train and get to know each other. It's a welcoming space for our customers (that's you!) and lends itself to the fun atmosphere that seems to be created over and over again with each class. And once all the 'wokking and rolling' (that's cooking) is over, it's a dedicated space to enjoy every morsel of food that we have created together, a chance for us all to sit down, share the feast, drink wine and be merry. At School of Wok, the ultimate aim is to learn lots, laugh more and share the Asian eating experience as it was intended to be – as a family.

HOW IT ALL STARTED

School of Wok began its life as a micro-business (just me) at a turning point in my life when I needed something to keep me going while I figured out my next move. The principles I held close when I started the cookery school meant much more to me than any job or career path I had taken over the last ten years. What I have learned over the course of a decade, alongside my friend and business partner Nev, is that life does not and should not revolve around business or work. However, given the impact the school has had on our lives, it has become hard for me not to treat School of Wok as an important member of my family.

I wasn't born with the idea I would grow up to become a wok chef, nor was I ever a natural reader or writer (my wife refers to me as the 'accidental writer'). These things all came with time, alongside an engrained dedication to travelling the world with my family, something taught to me by my parents and valued from a young age. My recipe writing has also evolved along the way as a response to our customers, from whom we have always gratefully received extensive feedback on anything we've ever offered. Between my first classes (chaotic but well-intentioned) and our classes of today (much more methodical and fine-tuned) lies a world of difference. This is something we've achieved bit by bit through feedback, success and a lot of 'Well, that didn't work, so let's try something else!'. This is a great approach when it comes to cooking, business or any aspect of life in general, and one I hope to continue to practise.

My expertise has not come simply through professional training, but from an upbringing built on my father's love of food and my mother's determination to make my sisters and I all confident learners, no matter what the subject. In the kitchen, my dad was the showman while my mum, the almighty tiger mum, would painstakingly prepare and chop everything to the finest slice, dice or matchstick to enable him to show off his flare. When School of Wok first opened, it was Mum who was prepping and chopping right there alongside me, taking on some of the workload so I could develop Dad's showmanship by finishing off the classes with a bit of finesse and leave customers with the desire for more. I am eternally grateful to my parents and the School of Wok team, who have stuck by me and kept the school going with a careful balance of good attributes, meticulous preparation and joyous flare.

DRAWING INSPIRATION FROM EVERYWHERE

In my previous books, I have focused solely on Chinese cuisine, representing my heritage. But the truth is, my diet and love of food has always been far more wide-ranging. Having grown up in the UK for the first decade of my life, home-cooked Chinese food was always part of my culinary DNA. Outside the family home, however, my knowledge and excitement around food and cooking ventured no further afield than that of my British friends – baked beans on toast and fish finger sandwiches were my dream dinners as a child. It wasn't until our move to Singapore when I was ten that my real food journey and culinary curiosity kicked in, influenced by the flavours in those areas of the world I was experiencing for the very first time.

In Singapore and Malaysia, no matter where the food culture originated, it's the locals' love of eating that has inspired the creation of such an array of tasty banquet and street food dishes, culminating in the wealth of delicious and varied national dishes. These cuisines offer fantastic examples of how two or three different cultures have infused their cooking techniques together, over a long period of time, to form something truly unique to a place. The local ingredients (whether Singaporean or Malay) offer naturally sweet, sour and savoury flavours, which are then complemented by the deep, earthy spices brought by the local Indian communities, then often married with the bold techniques of Chinese wok-based cooking. The culmination of flavours is sure to send you over the edge, which is one of our aims at School of Wok – to make it impossible for you *not* to use the new techniques or flavour profiles we teach you; they're just too enjoyable not to be cooked with and shared.

A JOURNEY INTO FLAVOUR BALANCING

The very first School of Wok website divided dishes up into familiar Western-style categories: Meat, Poultry, Fish and Seafood, Vegetables. This is not the traditional Asian way to divide up dishes on a menu, but having been brought up predominantly in the UK, I've always thought of menus, even Chinese menus, being categorized this way. When starting the school, it was simpler to split the classes or dishes up like a Western-based Chinese restaurant menu might. Over time, like many second or third generation immigrant kids, School of Wok class formats have veered closer to their origins. I stopped trying to work against them, and started splitting the classes into cuisines, teaching our students the art of balancing flavours, tastes and textures by cooking three or four dishes we believe work well together, like most Asian homes would.

A typical Asian dinner table is often filled to the brim with a variety of dishes showcasing a wide range of colours, textures and flavours. More often than not the dishes are conceived and cooked together to offer a balance of meat, fish and vegetables spread across the table. Our food is designed for sharing, so it's important to think of it in those terms. Rather than looking at the presentation of just one plate of food, I think a real understanding of how to create balance in Asian cuisine stems from the ability to zoom out and take a bird's eye view of the whole table – slow-braised dishes, flash-fried vegetables, colourful stir-fries and the gaps in the table filled in with bowls of steamed rice or platefuls of noodles. No matter the cuisine or culture and how our histories may differ, one thing shared by all the countries I have touched on in this book is that the final goal is a table full of food to be shared by all.

The book offers numerous recipes for fish, seafood, meat and vegetable dishes. When planning your meals, unless you're already cooking a noodle dish as the main carbohydrate for your meal, have in mind that a bowl of steamed rice and at least one or two dishes from the Tasty Sides chapter will work a treat to fill up your table and make your meals more balanced and wholesome. Think variety, think balance and you'll have the right mindset to put together a feast fit for a king, queen or just your rowdy, hungry Wednesday-night family.

It's hard to believe that it has taken ten years to write the first ever School of Wok cookbook. I hope that this book will provide you with some insight into the start of the School of Wok journey and its original inspiration: my parents. I also hope it offers useful advice to help support and inspire the future generation, nudging us to be playful with our kids' palates and plates, giving them time to explore the wonders that something as simple as a table full of food can bring. This book is a simple guide to the preparation required to perfect your wok cooking, and the pinch of finesse and flare that bring all of that hard work together. In Chinese, rarely do we say 'hello'. Rather, we greet each other by asking, 'Have you eaten yet?'. And the quickest way to sort out someone who hasn't eaten is definitely with a wok, so let's get wokking!

THE WOK CLOCK

The Wok Clock has found its way in and out of numerous classes and cooking demonstrations across the world. It's been referenced all over the internet and talked about in almost every TV show I have been lucky enough to take part in and I'm pretty sure it'll follow me way past retirement and beyond. It's such a simple and practical tool, a way of reminding yourself to be super-organized in the kitchen, and a way of releasing yourself from the chains of the cookbook while you're doing the actual cooking. For those new to the Wok Clock, let me explain how it works.

At School of Wok, we like to arrange our prepared ingredients in a systematic manner, using a round plate as a clock. This method is not exclusive to wok cooking (though the name was so catchy it just stuck); it can be used when organizing ingredients for all types of cooking at home, no matter the cuisine. Once you have prepared all your ingredients, arrange them around the plate in the order in which you'll need them, beginning at 12 o'clock and working your way around the plate clockwise. Whether you are cooking a stir-fry or a slower-cooked curry, or even setting up a long list of ingredients that need to be pounded with a pestle and mortar, it works well. As a rule of thumb, when stir-frying for example, you tend to start with the base ingredients (onions, garlic, ginger) and the harder vegetables, then move on to the meats or other proteins, followed by the sauce or braising liquid. It's that simple!

Where appropriate in this book, the Wok Clock method has been used as a simple guide to preparation so you're ready and organized before you start a recipe. Once you get in the habit of using a Wok Clock, you'll find every aspect of your cooking will become neater and more straightforward, freeing you up to relish the joys of preparing dishes and learning new cooking techniques without scampering around to consult every last sentence of the recipe and then losing the plot all together. Once you have cooked a recipe a few times and become familiar with this way of organizing, you can simply refer to the illustrated Wok Clocks to help you 'wok' your way through.

WOK'S IT ALL ABOUT?

Woks are often seen as simple bits of equipment with one major use: to stir-fry. Yet, the simplicity and speed of their use is often what makes cooking with one so difficult to perfect. At the end of the day, no matter the cuisine, cooking is all about understanding heat. Once you master that, becoming a domestic wok-master isn't actually as hard as you may think.

Many anthropologists and historians believe that the wok was invented over 2,000 years ago to help preserve the limited fuel and food supplies available at the time in Central and Eastern Asia and India. The design made it possible for a wider variety of dishes to be created from a limited range of ingredients and equipment at lightning speed. Woks were originally made from ceramic, but once the material changed and they became lighter in weight, woks became more portable and started to travel around the world with their owners.

Depending on how you define a wok (there is debate over whether to classify it merely by shape or also by the material used to make it), there are differing views as to the utensil's origins. However, one thing is for sure: the wok was designed as a 'one-pot-stop' that could be made in all different sizes for ease of sustaining families and communities and feeding the masses.

The word 'wok' can be translated literally from the Cantonese as 'cooking pot'. Given its portable nature and simple maintenance needs, there's little wonder the wok migrated to so many different parts of the world. I could argue that life hasn't changed much since the time of the Han Dynasty: just like back then, I for one have never really moved anywhere without taking my beloved wok with me. When I first arrived at university, I turned up with a wok and a bag of rice, which pretty much got me and my housemates through the first term. It's the wok's surface area and shape that lends itself to such versatility; it's an essential tool in many cuisines and cultures. In Japan it's called a *chūkanabe*, meaning 'Chinese pot'; in Malaysia it's a *kuali* or *kawah*, in India it's a *karahi*. Although they may differ slightly in size or structure, some with deeper sides than others, these wok-like vessels have all been created, adapted and used to achieve similar results: to utilize the available space, time, fuel and ingredients efficiently to feed and sustain a large group of people as well as possible.

TYPES OF WOK

Before the introduction of Western cookware (pots and pans) to Asia, a wok would have been used for all the different cooking techniques and can still be today, as we will see in this book.

From the seemingly rather fragile ceramic woks of the Han Dynasty, the wok evolved quite quickly to more robust cast-iron models, followed much later by carbon steel – the most popular and widely used material in today's modern version. Recently it has jumped an extra step in modernization with the addition of a nonstick layer for ease of cleaning. All equally versatile (as long as you know what you're doing), most of these types of wok can still be found in kitchen shops today.

There are numerous woks to choose from, which can be confusing for those who are just starting their wok journey. Hopefully these descriptions will help clear up that confusion and give you some confidence to choose the right one for you.

Round-Based Carbon Steel Woks

Woks were commonly shaped with a perfectly round bottom, designed to be used over the traditional Chinese pit-style hearth, similar to what we might see today in more commercial settings rather than domestic kitchens. This shape allows heat to be distributed evenly across the wok's base, creating a wider cooking surface and continual heat circulation during cooking. Most carbon steel woks (whether round- or flat-based) tend to be relatively thin in gauge to allow for quick changes in heat with just a simple flick or toss of the wok, making them perfect for stir-frying.

Professional chefs in Chinese restaurants often still use pit-like stoves, which give off a tremendous amount of heat and power. They have to master their *wok hei* or 'wok's air' to control the heat and create that smoky flavour that comes from a good wok-cooked stir-fry. My personal preference when it comes to wok shape is this type of round-based wok, especially when a hob permits you to sit your wok over the fire safely and securely, particularly with gas, open-flame cooking or specially designed induction hobs.

Flat-Based Carbon Steel Woks

The flat-based woks we are accustomed to seeing in shops worldwide were created much later as a response to the Western home kitchen. They are designed for use on flatter surfaces such as halogen, ceramic, electric and induction hobs. The original flat-based woks would have been hand-hammered into shape and then flipped inside out to form as smooth a finish on the inside as possible. Much like with round-based woks, the thinner the gauge of metal used to make a flat-based wok, the better it is for stir-frying. These days flat-based woks can be made from various materials that may feel a lot thicker; they won't necessarily be the best choice if you plan to use them mainly for stir-fries.

TIP A note, or rather a plea, if you're just beginning your wok journey: preparation and wok care is crucial for cooking success – and to do that you *must* season a carbon steel wok first before cooking with it (see page 16). Perhaps even more importantly, after use, you *must* dry it on a hob over a medium-high heat until it is bone dry, or else it will rust! You will find notes on seasoning woks and how to look after your carbon steel woks further on in this chapter. If you look after your carbon steel wok properly, it should get blacker and better as it ages, making your food even tastier with time.

Nonstick Woks

Most thin nonstick woks are essentially carbon steel woks covered with a nonstick coating for ease of use and cleaning. Unlike pure carbon steel woks, seasoning is not required, however it's likely that at some point you will have to replace your nonstick wok as excessive use creates wear and tear and nonstick coatings do not last a lifetime. I find that nonstick woks cannot withstand quite the same battering or high heat as traditional carbon steel woks. However, there are ways and means of keeping them going for longer if you are happy to persist until absolutely necessary to buy a new one. Always use wooden or silicone utensils with a nonstick wok and follow the same method you'd use to clean a carbon steel wok: boiling some water in a nonstick wok after cooking helps to gently remove food residue without damaging the coating. If the wok is not quite hot enough during cooking, or you unintentionally load too much into the wok, ingredients may still catch and stick despite the nonstick coating. Once boiled, though, any residue should slip off the nonstick coating to make cleaning easier.

Cast Iron & Thicker-Gauge Woks

Cast iron woks tend to be quite heavy and are therefore much harder to flick and toss, making them less suited to stir-frying. They are, however, perfect for slower-cooked and braised dishes such as curries and stews. The thicker base of a cast iron wok provides incredible heat distribution, which also makes them great for deep-frying. If you have a cast iron wok, there is no reason why you can't stir-fry in it too, just don't try to flick and toss the wok or you'll be in for an injury in no time! Instead, just use one or two spatulas and fold your ingredients through the wok gently, creating the same circulation of heat but without having your wrist pay the price. I recommend using a cast iron or thicker-based wok for the slower-cooked recipes in the book, although you could also use a thick-based saucepan or cast iron casserole pan if you're not planning on or don't have the space or budget to invest in more cookware. Do note that cast iron is also corrosive and so must be dried on the hob until bone dry, much like a carbon steel wok.

How to Season a Carbon Steel Wok

Seasoning your carbon steel wok is essential if you are going to go from wok novice to wok star. Most carbon steel woks come with an anti-rust layer to prevent them corroding in the shop. These days you can also find pre-seasoned carbon steel woks that avoid the need to season yourself, but such woks must still be cleaned and dried on the hob in exactly the same way as a classic carbon steel or cast iron wok. Unless pre-seasoned or coated with a nonstick layer in the factory, you need to season your wok before you use it for the first time to create a natural nonstick layer on the surface.

We created an incredibly useful series of videos on the School of Wok YouTube channel called 'Dr Wok Sessions'. They detail the seasoning and maintenance procedures for a carbon steel wok, aimed at anyone interested in cooking with these more traditional pieces of equipment. Much like a French skillet pan, if you maintain your carbon steel or cast iron wok well, it should last a lifetime and improve with age.

Follow the steps below to look after your wok and you may well be able to pass it down from generation to generation. You should only really need to season your wok once if you look after it properly from then on. However, if you happen to boil highly acidic ingredients (such as sauces with a large quantity of lemon juice or rice vinegar) in a carbon steel wok, it does run the risk of stripping off the layer of carbon that you have burned onto the surface through the seasoning process. Only then would you have to repeat this seasoning process to protect it again from future damage.

1. Give your wok a good scrub with a metal scourer.

2. Heat the wok over a high gas flame until a patch of dark grey-blue colour appears.

3. Repeat this heating process all the way around the wok so that the whole surface is grey-blue. Let the wok cool down.

4. Dab a thick, folded pad of kitchen paper into vegetable oil (about 1 tablespoon of oil will do). Apply the oil sparingly over the inside surface of the cool wok. Note: do not pour oil into the wok when it is hot as this could be dangerous. Completely polish the inside of the wok by rubbing the oil in a circular motion all around the inside surface.

5. Now heat the wok once more over a high heat until it starts to smoke. Keep heating until all the smoke disappears and the wok is a dark grey colour. It's now ready to use. The wok may have shimmers of other colours after you have seasoned it for the first time, but will become darker and blacker with further use.

How to Maintain a Wok

Rusty carbon steel and cast iron woks are a sad sight I often see when going to the dump. Caring for your wok after each use is just as important, if not more so, than seasoning the wok in the first place. If you do not wash and dry carbon steel or cast iron woks properly they will rust, as they are corrosive metals. The cleaning process is easy, so should be used repeatedly. Follow these steps to keep your wok going as long as possible.

1. To clean, half-fill the wok with hot water and place over a high heat.

2. Bring the water to a boil and boil vigorously to deglaze.

3. Clean thoroughly with a sponge or scourer, using a little detergent if necessary.

4. Always dry your carbon steel or cast iron wok on the hob. Place it over a high heat until all the water has evaporated and the wok is bone dry. Allow to cool completely before putting it away.

CIRCULATING HEAT & MASTERING *WOK HEI*

No matter what type of wok you use, if you understand how to circulate heat around your wok using a handful of different methods, you will be able to cook your food quickly, efficiently and effortlessly (well, mostly), while maintaining a high heat and without burning your food. To do this, you need to practice wok cooking and master *wok hei*, the art of controlling and moving the hot air around the wok, to infuse satisfying smoky flavours into your food without any sign of burning whatsoever. Manoeuvring heat around the wok should be done in circular motions, whether it's in the form of stirring, folding, flicking and tossing or shaking the ingredients. All these circular motions help you to take control of your *wok hei*.

When cooking at home, it's easy to be apprehensive about smoking-hot pans – especially if you have a sensitive smoke detector, children around or don't wish the entirety of your home to smell like a well-seasoned wok. However, when stir-frying or even braising with a wok, it's imperative to understand how and when to control and change heat, rather than fearing it, to improve your finished dishes.

Here are a few simple tips and tricks to help you to perfect your wok cooking:

Don't overfill your wok with ingredients as it will cool down dramatically. Most of the recipes in this book serve two people. If you need to serve more people by increasing the quantity of ingredients, I recommend frying all the vegetables first, then removing them from the wok. Next reheat the wok and sear the meat or other protein (if required), so as not to overfill the wok. Once your protein has seared, return the vegetables to the wok to finish your stir-fry. This is not as crucial when it comes to curries or slower-cooked dishes, but imperative for the quicker cooks.

Bringing your wok back to a high heat at various points in a recipe is crucial to understanding *wok hei*. When stir-frying, for example, you will often notice in the recipes that I recommend heating the wok to smoking point before adding the sauce. This allows the sauce to bubble up and caramelize immediately. It's a technique that is just as useful when braising in a wok too.

***Wok hei* isn't just about high heat**, it's about knowing when to increase your heat in order to sear your ingredients immediately, but then allow them enough time to cook through without the risk of burning. To help with your wok confidence, there are a few easy ways to cool the wok down:

1. Stirring: Use your ladle or spatula to stir the ingredients around the wok. This will cool your wok down slightly and keep the heat circulating to help prevent ingredients from burning.

2. Folding: Get underneath your ingredients with a spatula or use several short flicks of the wrist holding the wok handle to fold them over themselves several times. Use a quick, circular motion to help cool your wok and create a more vertical circulation of heat. This technique is the simplest way to flick your ingredients around the wok and introduce cooler air.

3. Wok toss: Without being too 'show boaty' (overly dramatic), give your wok a long push forwards and a quick flick backwards, as if flipping a pancake in a pan. If you fancy trying this wok trick, tie a couple of knots into a clean tea towel, place it in a cool wok off the heat and practise the toss. If the tea towel flips over, you've got the knack! This method will introduce cooler air into the wok very quickly, which is why it's such an efficient way to circulate heat once mastered. (Bonus side effect: it looks really cool!)

4. Tummy and head movement: Give your wok a vigorous shake, while creating a stirring motion in the centre of your wok with your ladle or spatula at the same time. This method is often used when trying to spread sauces evenly through dishes and for this reason is particularly useful when stir-frying noodles. This is more of a horizontal circulation of heat that draws gushes of cooler air into the ingredients.

Never lose your sizzle. Although it's important to master ways to cool your wok down (see above), it's just as important to remember to bring it back up to heat every time you add in a new ingredient when stir-frying. Once you have circulated the air around your wok for a few seconds, the high-heat cooking needs to continue until sauces have been caramelized to your desired texture and the ingredients are well cooked. Don't risk stir-boiling your food when you should be stir-frying; it will make all the difference to your cooking and the success of the dish.

HOW TO STEAM IN A WOK

No matter which technique you are using, wok cooking shouldn't require excessive amounts of equipment – just a few key pieces will suffice. There are numerous ways to steam food in a wok but probably the easiest is with a bamboo steamer basket. The bigger domestic steamers are around 25cm (10 inches) in diameter and are great for steaming dumplings, baos, fillets of fish or anything else that can sit in a heatproof bowl or plate that fits inside the steamer. Fill the wok about one-third of the way up the sides with boiling water and place the steamer in the wok with the food inside, making sure the water does not touch the steamer. Cover the steamer with its lid and keep the water gently simmering during cooking.

When steaming a whole fish or something that needs to sit on a bigger plate, I use a more makeshift steamer set-up using the wok and the wok lid. This alternative method is a great way to improvise using equipment that you probably already have in your kitchen. Start with your wok, filled one-third of the way up the sides with boiling water. Place a heatproof bowl in the middle of the wok, protruding just above the surface of the water, followed by a heatproof plate (for your food to sit on) on top of the bowl. Make sure your plate isn't too large: there should be space in between the plate and the wok's edges to allow you to pick it up and there must also be enough room for the steam to rise up around the food. Use a domed wok lid to sit on top of the wok if you have one, otherwise a large flat lid will work at a pinch.

HOW TO DEEP-FRY IN A WOK

Woks are perfect for deep-frying as their large surface area allows you more room for ingredients. If using a wok to deep-fry, I'd highly recommend using a flat-based wok on a flat hob so that you are frying in the safest possible way!

Half-fill (no more) your wok with vegetable oil and heat to the desired temperature. Test the temperature of your oil by placing the tip of a wooden implement, such as a skewer or chopstick, into the oil. If the wood starts to fizz after a second or so, the oil has reached around 180°C (350°F). If the wood starts to fizz after 3–4 seconds, it has reached 170°C (335°F). If the oil is too hot and fizzes up too quickly, then switch off the heat for a few minutes before starting to fry anything. Filling up your wok with ingredients will bring the temperature down quite quickly anyway.

Once the oil has reached the desired temperature, carefully place your ingredients into the wok using a slotted spoon or frying nest. At School of Wok, we tend to use a traditional frying 'spider', with a bamboo handle and wire mesh bowl that allows you to pick food from the wok without collecting any residual oil. You can purchase these if desired on our School of Wok website.

TIPS FOR DEEP-FRYING

1. Never overfill your wok with oil. It can rise up when you add the ingredients you want to deep-fry and may overflow, especially when frying wetter items which will spit.

2. Don't overcrowd the wok with too many ingredients, or you will reduce the temperature of the oil. It's best to deep-fry in batches so the food comes out crispier rather than soaking up oil and becoming soggy.

3. If you do have to fry your ingredients in batches and are worried that your first batch will have gone cold by the time you have finished cooking the last batch, re-fry all of the ingredients for a minute or so at the end after the initial cooking is complete. Alternatively, pop your oven on at 110°C (225°F), Gas Mark ¼, and place the cooked food on a baking tray in the oven to keep warm until you've finished with the last batch and are ready to serve.

CHINESE

I am often asked about the key to cooking great Chinese food. While there are many different cooking techniques to master, a sense of balance is perhaps the most important thing. When cooking any type of Chinese food, balancing flavour, texture and colour is what creates the perfect meal. I talk a lot about flavour balance and you will start to notice that keeping an eye on ratios and combinations of certain sauces or ingredients will help to create it. However, something perhaps less familiar in home cooking is how to balance texture. Wok cooking lends itself to enhancing the natural textures of ingredients. Stir-frying meat creates crisp outer edges and succulent tenderness. Steaming vegetables or fish uses gentle heat to seal in flavours while allowing the ingredients to stand proud in their shape – fish fillets hold their flakiness, vegetables retain their natural bite.

The Chinese pantry can be extensive to say the least. I could happily spend hours, if not days, in a Chinese supermarket, getting lost in curiosity among the ingredients – many of which I still have no idea how to use. The simplest way to start with the Chinese pantry is to split up the flavour profiles, making sure that you have at least one sauce to touch five of the six parts of the palate. For example, light soy sauce for saltiness, oyster sauce or vegetarian stir-fry sauce for a base of savoury, a chilli oil or chilli bean sauce for spiciness, rice vinegar to add a hint of sour here or there, and sugar to balance out the sour with sweetness. If you dare to push into the more bitter side of your palate (a flavour profile we learn to enjoy as we get older), you might enjoy exploring Chinese teas or special dried leaves and herbs, or add a pinch from a pot of Chinese five spice powder to create a longer, lingering bitter finish and flavour. You can also (and I would encourage this) separate out Chinese five spices to craft and create your own blends, or to use individually – star anise, cinnamon, fennel seeds, cloves, bay leaves and various different peppercorns. (Although titles of Chinese ingredients are usually quite literal, five spice blends can often have a mix of up to ten ingredients.) These are some of the foundations of the apothecary that is the Chinese home kitchen, alongside the essential fresh ingredients of ginger, garlic, spring onions and chillies, not to be forgotten. However many spices you end up using, just bear in mind how strong, fragrant and sometimes potent, they can be and use them sparingly so as not to overpower your dish.

Special wok utensils are a godsend and make wok cooking that much more enjoyable and leisurely. If you cook a lot of stir-fries or use your wok more than three times a week, I would highly recommend getting a wok ladle and spatula to elevate and improve your Chinese cooking. These wok-specific implements have a slightly more obtuse angle at the neck which allows you to push and fold ingredients seamlessly around the wok, continuously circulating the heat. These little details make all the difference, especially when it comes to rapid-fire cooking.

My advice is to stock your pantry and equipment drawers quite simply to start with, and then build as you go. Pick one or two dishes to cook and perfect, then add on. Before you know it, you will find that perfect balance of flavour, texture and colour which will allow you to extend your range and grasp what it means to make truly great Chinese food.

DRY-FRIED SICHUAN BEEF

PREP: 15 MINS | COOK: 6 MINS | SERVES 2

300g (10½oz) rib-eye
  or rump steak, cut against
  the grain into 3–4cm
  (1¼–1½ inch) batons
½ teaspoon Sichuan
  peppercorns
½ thumb-sized piece of
  ginger, peeled and cut
  into matchsticks
2 spring onions,
  cut into matchsticks
½ leek, cut into matchsticks
1 carrot, cut into 3–4cm
  (1¼–1½ inch) batons
2 celery sticks, cut into
  3–4cm (1¼–1½ inch) batons
vegetable oil
steamed rice, to serve

SAUCE

2 tablespoons chilli bean sauce
  (*toban jiang*)
½ teaspoon Lao Gan Ma
  chilli oil (swapsies: Chiu
  Chow chilli oil)
2 tablespoons Shaoxing rice
  wine (swapsies: dry sherry)
½ tablespoon light soy sauce
½ teaspoon sesame oil

MARINADE

¼ teaspoon salt
¼ teaspoon sugar
½ teaspoon sesame oil

This dish may take some getting used to if you're not accustomed to the tingling, citrus feeling that Sichuan peppercorns leave on your tongue. Consider it the older, more mature cousin of deep-fried takeaway-style chilli beef (which is also tasty, but not for the same occasion).

1. Mix the sauce ingredients together in a small bowl. Place the beef into a separate bowl and massage the marinade ingredients well into the meat. Grind the Sichuan peppercorns using a pestle and mortar or spice grinder.

2. **Build Your Wok Clock:** Start at 12 o'clock with the steak, followed by the ginger and spring onions, ground Sichuan peppercorns, the bowl of sauce, then the leek, the carrot and lastly the celery.

3. Heat 1 tablespoon of vegetable oil in the wok to a high heat. Add in the steak and stir-fry for 1–2 minutes until each piece is browned and slightly crisp around the edges. Transfer the beef to a plate and carefully give the wok a clean with kitchen paper if there is any meat stuck to the bottom. If not, carry straight on and return the wok to the hob on a high heat.

4. Now place the ginger and spring onions into the wok and stir-fry for 30 seconds. Add the Sichuan pepper and then immediately pour in the sauce. At this point, reduce the heat to medium and then add the leek, carrot and celery to the wok, stir-frying for 30 seconds between each additional ingredient. Bring to a vigorous boil and then return the steak to the pan and cook for a further 1–2 minutes, coating the meat fully with the sauce. Serve with steamed rice on the side.

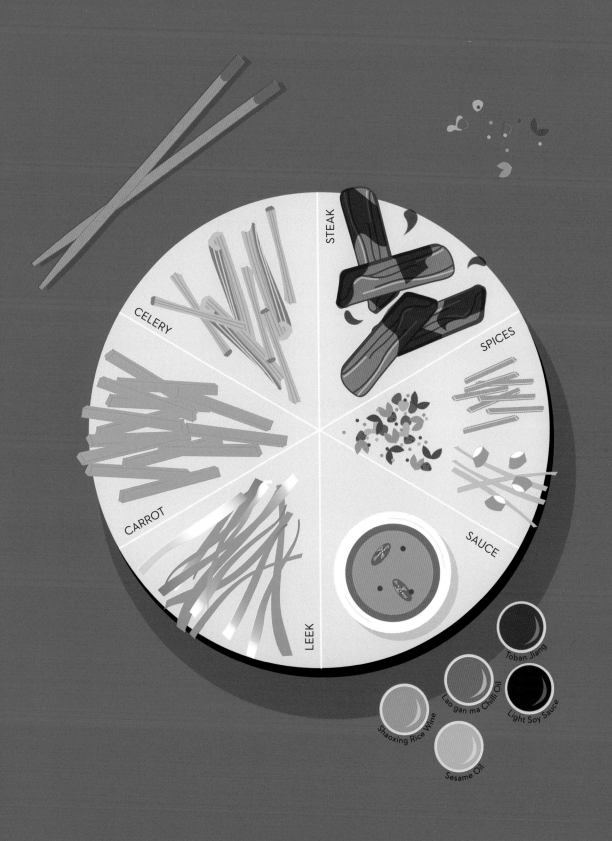

STEAK

CELERY

SPICES

CARROT

SAUCE

LEEK

Toban Jiang

Lao gan ma Chilli Oil

Light Soy Sauce

Shaoxing Rice Wine

Sesame Oil

GENERAL TSO'S CHICKEN

PREP: 25 MINS | COOK: 15 MINS | SERVES 2

10 dried red chillies
300g (10½oz) skinless,
    boneless chicken thighs,
    diced
200g (7oz) cornflour, seasoned
    with ¼ teaspoon salt and
    ¼ teaspoon pepper
½ thumb-sized piece of ginger,
    peeled and finely sliced
2 garlic cloves, finely sliced
2 spring onions, finely sliced
vegetable oil

SAUCE

30g (1oz) sugar
1 teaspoon sriracha chilli sauce
1 tablespoon sweet chilli sauce
1 tablespoon oyster sauce
½ tablespoon black rice
    vinegar
1 tablespoon light soy sauce
½ teaspoon dark soy sauce
50ml (2fl oz) water

MARINADE

1 teaspoon sesame oil
½ teaspoon sugar
1 tablespoon light soy sauce
1 egg, lightly beaten

TO SERVE

sliced red chilli
sliced spring onions
steamed rice
flash-fried green vegetables

Why is General Tso so popular? Well, this dish is sweet, sour, spicy and savoury with just the right amount of salty. It's the perfect balance of flavour, texture and colour and a wonderful place to start your wok journey.

1. Soak the dried red chillies in hot water for 10 minutes, then drain. Mix the sauce ingredients together in a small bowl.

2. Place the chicken in a mixing bowl and massage the marinade ingredients into the meat. Then pour the seasoned cornflour over the chicken and massage until each piece of meat separates and has a dry dusty white coating.

3. **Build Your Wok Clock:** Start at 12 o'clock with your bowl of cornflour-coated chicken, followed by the ginger, garlic and spring onions, the soaked red chillies, then lastly the sauce.

4. Deep-fry the coated chicken in vegetable oil at 180°C (350°F) for 4–5 minutes until golden brown (see page 21). Transfer the chicken to a plate lined with kitchen paper.

5. If using your wok for deep-frying, carefully pour out the oil into a heatproof bowl to cool and give your wok a quick wipe with kitchen paper. Place the wok back on the hob and bring 1 tablespoon of vegetable oil to a high heat. Add in your ginger, garlic and spring onions and stir-fry for 30 seconds.

6. Next add the dried chillies, followed immediately by the sauce mixture. Bring the sauce to a vigorous boil for 3–4 minutes until syrupy, then add the deep-fried meat, tossing the wok a few times so that the sauce fully coats the chicken. Sprinkle with sliced red chilli and spring onions and serve immediately with steamed rice and flash-fried green veg.

CHILLI OIL NOODLES

PREP: 5 MINS | COOK: 6 MINS | SERVES 2

2–3 garlic cloves, finely chopped
¼ thumb-sized piece of ginger,
    peeled and finely chopped
½ spring onion, finely chopped
vegetable oil
200g (7oz) flat wheat noodles,
    fine wheat noodles or
    soba noodles
generous handful of
    torn coriander

CHILLI OIL
2 tablespoons Lao Gan Ma
    chilli oil (swapsies: Chiu
    Chow chilli oil)
1 tablespoon light soy sauce
½ teaspoon dark soy sauce
½ teaspoon Chingkiang
    vinegar, or rice vinegar
1 teaspoon toasted
    sesame seeds

My dad used to tell me stories about his childhood growing up in refugee camps in Hong Kong. For him, a plain bowl of rice or noodles could be transformed into a banquet with just a teaspoon or two of chilli oil. Simple dishes like this follow the exact same principle and lend themselves to a quick snack or a mid-week meal with no fuss.

1. Mix together the chilli oil ingredients in a bowl.

2. **Build Your Wok Clock:** Start at 12 o'clock with the garlic and ginger, followed by the spring onion and lastly the chilli oil.

3. Heat 2 tablespoons of vegetable oil in a wok over a medium heat, then add the garlic and ginger. Stir-fry for 30–60 seconds until fragrant. Remove from the heat, add in the spring onions and the chilli oil and stir well.

4. Bring a pot of water to a boil and add the noodles. Boil for 4–5 minutes or according to the packet instructions, until tender. Drain through a sieve then tip into a large bowl.

5. Pour the chilli oil mixture over the top of the noodles and add the coriander. Mix thoroughly to coat each strand of noodle with sauce, divide into bowls and serve.

PEKING MANDARIN PORK

PREP: 15 MINS | COOK: 13 MINS | SERVES 2

2 pork chops or shoulder steaks
½ thumb-sized piece of ginger,
    peeled and roughly chopped
2 garlic cloves, roughly chopped
1 spring onion, cut into 2cm
    (¾ inch) chunks
3 star anise
1 small cinnamon stick
vegetable oil
handful of coriander leaves,
    to garnish

MARINADE
½ teaspoon salt
½ teaspoon Chinese five spice
¼ teaspoon sugar
1 tablespoon Shaoxing rice wine
    (swapsies: dry sherry)
1 teaspoon sesame oil
4 tablespoons cornflour

SAUCE
½ tablespoon orange
    marmalade
100ml (3½fl oz) fresh
    orange juice
1 tablespoon rice vinegar
1 tablespoon plum sauce
    (swapsies: ketchup)
1 tablespoon light soy sauce
1 teaspoon dark soy sauce
100ml (3½fl oz) chicken stock

Deep-fried meats don't have to just be crispy. If you know what you're doing, you can use the cooking technique to create a range of textures. In this dish, the sparing use of cornflour creates a crisped edge around each piece of pork, at the same time allowing it to soak up plenty of the moreish sweet and sour sauce.

1. Carefully, using the back of your knife or cleaver, bash the pork chops or steaks to tenderize the meat, then cut into 3–4cm (1¼–1½ inch) pieces and place in a mixing bowl. Massage the marinade ingredients into the pork, taking care to add in the cornflour at the very end and mix well. Mix the sauce ingredients together in a small bowl.

2. **Build Your Wok Clock:** Start at 12 o'clock with the marinated pork, followed by the ginger, garlic and spring onion, star anise and cinnamon stick, and lastly the sauce bowl.

3. Deep-fry the pork in vegetable oil in 2 batches at 180°C (350°F) for 4–5 minutes until golden brown (see page 21). Transfer the pork to a plate lined with kitchen paper.

4. If using your wok for deep-frying, carefully pour out the oil into a heatproof bowl to cool and give your wok a quick wipe with kitchen paper. Place the wok back on the hob and bring ½ tablespoon of vegetable oil to a high heat until smoking hot. Add the ginger, garlic and spring onion to the wok and stir-fry for 30–60 seconds before adding the star anise and cinnamon stick. Next add the sauce to the wok and bring to a vigorous boil. Once bubbling rapidly, add the fried pieces of pork into the sauce and vigorously boil for a further 1–2 minutes. Garnish with coriander and serve.

GARLIC & VERMICELLI STEAMED PRAWNS

PREP: 20 MINS | COOK: 5 MINS | SERVES 2

12–15 shell-on raw river
    shrimp or tiger prawns
2 spring onions,
    cut into matchsticks
1 large red chilli,
    cut into matchsticks
1 nest of mung bean
    glass vermicelli
3–4 tablespoons ready-made
    crispy fried garlic or shallots

GARLIC OIL
1 head of garlic, cloves
    separated and finely chopped
3 tablespoons vegetable oil

SAUCE
2 tablespoons light soy sauce
1 teaspoon sugar
3 tablespoons boiling water

This combination of techniques is common to many Chinese cuisines. Steaming preserves the delicate flavours and textures of seafood and fish, while the hot oil sizzle gives an immediate tempering of herbs and spices to bring out their essential oils, flavour and vibrant colour.

1. Butterfly the prawns by cutting through the shells down the backs, slicing straight through the heads and running your knife through the meat to open them out. Stop slicing just before the tail to keep it intact. Scrape out the black digestive cord, then place the butterflied prawns in a mixing bowl and wash well in cold water.

2. For the garlic oil, place the garlic in a heatproof bowl. Heat the vegetable oil in a small pan until smoking hot, then pour the oil over the chopped garlic to sizzle.

3. Place the spring onion and red chilli matchsticks into a bowl of ice-cold water to allow them to curl. Mix the sauce ingredients together in a small bowl. Soak the vermicelli in boiling water for 3 minutes.

4. **Build Your Wok Clock:** Start at 12 o'clock with the bowl of vermicelli, followed by the prawns, the garlic oil (with garlic), the crispy fried garlic or shallots, the bowl of spring onion and chilli curls, and lastly the bowl of sauce.

5. Drain the vermicelli and place in a large shallow heatproof bowl. Place the prawns on top and spread all the garlic and oil over the butterflied prawns. Steam the bowl of vermicelli and prawns for 5 minutes (see page 20) until the prawn shells are coral pink in colour and the prawns are cooked.

6. Remove the lid and scatter the crispy fried garlic or shallots all over the prawns along with the drained curls of spring onion and chilli. Lastly pour the sauce over the top and serve.

GINGER & SPRING ONION CHICKEN

PREP: 15 MINS | COOK: 6 MINS | SERVES 2

300g (10½oz) skinless, boneless chicken thighs, diced
3-4 spring onions, roughly chopped
1 thumb-sized piece of ginger, peeled and cut into matchsticks
2 garlic cloves, roughly chopped
1 red onion, diced
1 green pepper, cored, deseeded and diced
vegetable oil
finely sliced spring onion, to garnish
steamed rice, to serve

MARINADE

1 teaspoon sesame oil
1 teaspoon sugar
pinch of Chinese five spice
1 tablespoon light soy sauce
1 tablespoon cornflour

SAUCE

1½ tablespoons oyster sauce
½ teaspoon dark soy sauce
2 capfuls of Shaoxing rice wine (swapsies: dry sherry)
50ml (2fl oz) chicken stock
½ teaspoon sesame oil

This is the type of cooking my sisters and I would have growing up, while our friends were feasting on fish finger sandwiches and baked beans on toast. I thank my mum for bringing such tasty, yet simple flavours to the dinner table every day.

1. Place the chicken in a mixing bowl and massage the marinade ingredients well into the meat, leaving the cornflour until last. Mix the sauce ingredients together in a small bowl.

2. **Build Your Wok Clock:** Start at 12 o'clock with the spring onions, ginger and garlic, followed by the red onion and pepper, the marinated chicken and lastly the sauce.

3. Heat 1 tablespoon of vegetable oil in a wok to a high heat. Once smoking hot, add the spring onions, ginger and garlic and stir-fry for 30-60 seconds. Push them to the edge of the wok and add the onion and pepper and continue to stir-fry for a further 30 seconds. Then, push all the vegetables to the edge of the wok (this will stop them from burning!) and bring the wok to a smoking point.

4. Add another 1 tablespoon of vegetable oil to the wok and bring to a high heat. Once smoking hot, place the marinated chicken into the wok and sear well for 30-60 seconds, then turn the meat over and repeat the searing on the other side. Now fold the vegetables over the top of the meat to stop them from burning. Count to 10 to bring all the ingredients up to a high heat, then pour the sauce around the edges so that it trickles down into the bowl of the wok and boils vigorously. Fold the ingredients through and finish off by stir-frying for 1-2 minutes. Sprinkle with finely sliced spring onion and serve with steamed rice.

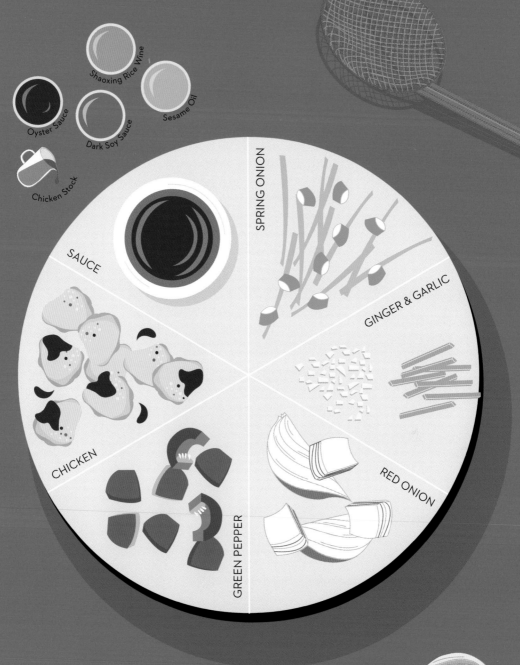

Shaoxing Rice Wine

Oyster Sauce

Dark Soy Sauce

Sesame Oil

Chicken Stock

SAUCE

SPRING ONION

GINGER & GARLIC

RED ONION

GREEN PEPPER

CHICKEN

XINJIANG CUMIN LAMB

PREP: 15 MINS, PLUS MARINATING | COOK: 8 MINS | SERVES 2

300g (10½oz) lamb rump steak,
    leg or neck, cut into 3cm
    (1¼ inch) cubes
handful of coriander
½ red onion, finely sliced
1 thumb-sized piece of ginger,
    peeled and finely chopped
6 garlic cloves, finely chopped
vegetable oil

MARINADE
½ teaspoon ground cumin
1 tablespoon light soy sauce
1 tablespoon Shaoxing rice wine
    (swapsies: dry sherry)
½ teaspoon sugar
1 tablespoon cornflour

DRY SPICES
1 teaspoon Sichuan peppercorns
2 teaspoons ground cumin
1 teaspoon chilli flakes (optional)
pinch of sea salt flakes

Lamb and goat meat are more commonly found on Chinese menus than you might think. This dish is hugely influenced by the cuisine of the Uyghur, a Muslim community from the northwest region of China. The flavour combination of soy and mild spices such as cumin is a match made in heaven, and complements the deep savoury flavours of the meat. I've written the recipe as a stir-fry, but the meat could easily be skewered and cooked directly over the coals on a barbecue. If you're using lamb leg or neck, you should marinate the meat overnight for more tender results.

1. Place the lamb in a mixing bowl and massage the marinade ingredients well into the meat. If using lamb leg or neck, cover and leave to marinate for a minimum of 45 minutes or overnight. For lamb rump steaks, 10–15 minutes will suffice.

2. Pick the coriander leaves off the stalks and roughly chop the stalks, keeping leaves and stalks separate. Grind the Sichuan peppercorns using a pestle and mortar or a spice grinder, then mix all the dry spices together in a small bowl.

3. **Build Your Wok Clock:** Start at 12 o'clock with your bowl of marinated lamb, followed by the red onion, ginger, garlic, coriander stalks and lastly the dry spices.

4. Heat 2–3 tablespoons of vegetable oil in the wok over a high heat until smoking hot. Once smoking hot, place your marinated meat into the hot oil and sear well for 30–60 seconds before turning. Turn the pieces of lamb and then sear the other side. Stir-fry the lamb for a further 1–2 minutes until browned on all sides, then transfer to a plate, saving any excess oil in the wok.

5. Place the wok back on a high heat and add the onion, then the ginger, garlic and coriander stalks one ingredient at a time, stir-frying for 30 seconds between each addition. Add the dry spices and the seared lamb. Continue to stir-fry for 1–2 minutes until fragrant and well combined. Garnish generously with the coriander leaves and serve.

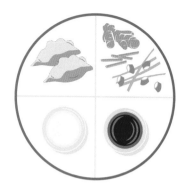

4 eggs
¼ teaspoon salt
½ teaspoon sesame oil
vegetable oil
½ thumb-sized piece of ginger,
    peeled and finely sliced
1 spring onion, cut into
    2–3cm (¾–1¼ inch) chunks,
    plus extra slices to garnish
2 teaspoons cornflour mixed
    with 2 teaspoons water
sliced red chilli, to garnish

FILLING

1 garlic clove, finely chopped
1 spring onion, finely chopped
1 carrot, finely chopped
handful of shiitake mushrooms,
    finely chopped
handful of kale, cabbage or
    Chinese leaf, finely chopped
100g (3½oz) minced pork,
    or finely chopped tofu
    or prawns (optional)
¼ teaspoon salt
pinch of black pepper
½ teaspoon sugar
1 teaspoon sesame oil

SAUCE

1 tablespoon oyster sauce
    or vegetarian stir-fry sauce
1 tablespoon light soy sauce
dash of dark soy sauce
300ml (½ pint) chicken
    or vegetable stock

BRAISED EGG DUMPLINGS

PREP: 20 MINS | COOK: 30 MINS | SERVES 2

You can fill these dumplings with anything that takes your fancy. Like other types of dumplings, this is a fantastic and delicious way to use up leftovers in your fridge. The egg dumplings are simply like mini omelettes or crêpes, stuffed with whatever you fancy throwing in there. Just chop the filling up nice and fine to avoid piercing the dumpling skins.

1. In a small jug, lightly beat the eggs and season with the salt and sesame oil. Place all the filling ingredients in a mixing bowl and mix thoroughly. Mix the sauce ingredients together in a small bowl.

2. Heat 1 tablespoon of vegetable oil in a frying pan to a medium heat. Pour 1–2 tablespoons of beaten egg into the pan and try to keep it contained in one spot so you can repeat to make several oval-shaped omelettes at the same time. At this point, reduce the heat to low so that the egg doesn't cook too quickly. Spoon 1 teaspoon of the filling into the centre of each partially cooked omelette then fold the egg in half over the filling and press the sides of the semi-circle with the back of a spatula to seal the edges. Repeat these steps, dotting several dumplings around your pan at a time, until all the egg and filling has been used. Set the dumplings aside on a plate.

3. **Build Your Wok Clock:** Start at 12 o'clock with the ginger and spring onion, then the sauce bowl, cornflour paste and finally the dumplings.

4. Heat 1 tablespoon of vegetable oil in your wok over a medium heat. Gently fry the sliced ginger and chunks of spring onion until the ginger is a golden brown. Then pour the sauce into the wok and bring to the boil. Once boiling, add the cornflour paste to the sauce and stir well; boil for a minute or so before reducing the heat to low. One by one, gently place each egg dumpling into the sauce and then boil for 8–10 minutes. Serve garnished with rings of red chilli and spring onion.

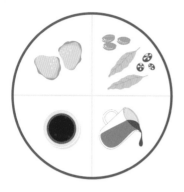

SICHUANESE MOUTH-WATERING CHICKEN

PREP: 25 MINS | COOK: 18 MINS | SERVES 2

1–1.5 litres (1¾–2½ pints)
  chicken stock
3–4 tablespoons Shaoxing rice
  wine (swapsies: dry sherry)
4 corn-fed chicken thighs,
  with skin and bone
3–4 tablespoons salted roasted
  peanuts, ground, plus extra
  to garnish
4 spring onions, finely chopped,
  to serve
handful of coriander leaves,
  to serve

CHILLI OIL
½ thumb-sized piece of ginger,
  peeled and finely chopped
½ tablespoon Sichuan peppercorns
½ teaspoon ground cumin
1½ teaspoons chilli flakes
½ teaspoon Chinese five spice
2 tablespoons sesame seeds
6–8 tablespoons vegetable oil

SAUCE
3 tablespoons light soy sauce
2 tablespoons sugar
1 teaspoon tomato purée
½ tablespoon Chinkiang vinegar,
  or rice vinegar
3 garlic cloves, finely chopped
1 thumb-sized piece of ginger,
  peeled and finely chopped
1–2 spring onions, finely chopped

STOCK AROMATICS
¼ thumb-sized piece of ginger,
  finely sliced
4 dried red chillies, chopped
2 bay leaves, chopped

The direct translation of the Chinese name for this dish is actually 'saliva chicken', which goes to show that literal translations can have their flaws. Although, you'll need luck trying to keep control of your saliva once you've dished this up – it's the epitome of mouth-watering.

1. For the chilli oil, pound all the ingredients, except the sesame seeds and oil, into a smooth paste using a pestle and mortar. Stir in the sesame seeds. Heat the vegetable oil in a small pan until smoking hot, then pour over the spices and mix well.

2. Mix 3–4 tablespoons of this chilli oil and all the sauce ingredients together in a small bowl. Place the stock aromatics together in a separate bowl.

3. **Build Your Wok Clock:** Start at 12 o'clock with the stock aromatics, followed by the chicken stock, rice wine and the chicken thighs.

4. Heat your wok over a medium heat and add the stock aromatics to release their aromas. Keep on the heat for 30–60 seconds, then pour chicken stock into the wok until it is two-thirds full. Add the Shaoxing rice wine, then place the chicken thighs in and bring to a boil. Once boiling, reduce the heat to medium and simmer for 15 minutes. Turn the heat off and leave the chicken in the hot stock for a further 5 minutes. Transfer the chicken to a bowl of cold water to stop it overcooking.

5. Just before serving, take the chicken off the bone and chop into 1cm (½ inch) slices. Place the chicken slices on a serving plate and top with 4–5 tablespoons of sauce. Add the ground peanuts to the remaining sauce to soak up the flavour, then pour over the top of the chicken. Sprinkle the dish with some extra ground peanuts, finely chopped spring onions and coriander.

VEGAN CHOW MEIN

PREP: 15 MINS, PLUS SOAKING & DRYING | COOK: 7 MINS | SERVES 2

200g (7oz) chow mein
    wheat noodles
100g (3½oz) firm tofu,
    cut into 1–2cm (½–¾ inch)
    thick batons
½ onion, sliced
3–4 Tenderstem broccoli spears,
    cut into long diagonal lengths
½ red pepper, sliced
1 head of pak choi, sliced
1 spring onion, finely sliced
vegetable oil

MARINADE
1 teaspoon light soy sauce
½ teaspoon sugar
½ teaspoon sesame oil

SAUCE
1 tablespoon vegan stir-fry
    sauce, such as mushroom
1 tablespoon light soy sauce
1 tablespoon dark soy sauce
1 teaspoon sugar
1 tablespoon sesame oil

This classic favourite is traditionally cooked with egg noodles and strips of meat, but this is a vegan version. Take your time to fry the tofu until golden brown on all sides before continuing the stir-fry to add texture to the dish. You won't miss the meat.

1. Soak the noodles in hot water for 3–4 minutes until they lose their packet shape. Drain them through a sieve and leave to dry on a clean tea towel for 10–15 minutes. Place the tofu in a bowl and then gently massage the marinade ingredients into it. Mix the sauce ingredients together in a small bowl.

2. **Build Your Wok Clock:** Start at 12 o'clock with the bowl of marinated tofu, followed by the onion, broccoli, red pepper, pak choi, spring onion, noodles and then lastly the sauce.

3. Heat 4–5 tablespoons of vegetable oil in your wok to a medium-high heat. Add the tofu and cook for 1–2 minutes, turning regularly, until golden brown on all sides. Transfer the tofu to a plate.

4. Pour off any excess oil into a heatproof bowl and bring the wok back to high heat with ½ tablespoon of vegetable oil. Add the onion, then the broccoli, red pepper, pak choi and spring onion, stir-frying for 30 seconds between each additional ingredient. Once all the vegetables are in the wok, bring the wok to a smoking point and then add your noodles. Stir-fry for 30–60 seconds until well mixed.

5. Then, keeping the heat high, pour the sauce into the wok. Give your wok a vigorous shake while stirring with your ladle or spatula (like a 'tummy and head' movement, see page 19) to help distribute the sauce evenly throughout the noodles. Continue to stir-fry for 1–2 minutes until the sauce evenly coats all the ingredients and then serve immediately.

Sugar

Vegan Stir-fry Sauce

Sesame Oil

Dark Soy Sauce

Light Soy Sauce

SAUCE

TOFU

ONION

BROCCOLI

RED PEPPER

PAK CHOI

SPRING ONION

NOODLES

TAIWANESE POPCORN CHICKEN

PREP: 10 MINS | COOK: 12 MINS | SERVES 2

300g (10½oz) skinless, boneless
    chicken thighs, cut into 2cm
    (¾ inch) pieces
200g (7oz) cornflour
vegetable oil
handful of Thai basil leaves

SEASONING
1 teaspoon Sichuan peppercorns
1 teaspoon black peppercorns
1 teaspoon sea salt flakes

MARINADE
2 garlic cloves, finely chopped
¼ thumb-sized piece of ginger,
    peeled and finely chopped
½ teaspoon salt
½ teaspoon sugar
pinch of white pepper
½ teaspoon Chinese five spice
1 tablespoon Shaoxing rice wine
    (swapsies: dry sherry)
1 tablespoon light soy sauce

Full recipe credit here goes to one of our lovely chef tutors, Emma Chung, for this wonderfully crispy Taiwanese street food staple. Emma's detailed explanations and seamless cooking talent have recently led her to join our School of Wok YouTube channel, and this is one of her best dishes yet. It's crispy chicken, in bite-sized pieces, tossed with fried herbs and spicy salt – what's not to like?

1. Grind the seasoning ingredients using a pestle and mortar or spice grinder. Place the chicken in a mixing bowl and massage the marinade ingredients into the meat. Pour the cornflour over the chicken and massage until each piece of meat separates and has a dusty white coating.

2. Deep-fry the coated chicken in vegetable oil in 2–3 batches at 180°C (350°F) (see page 21). Cook each batch for 3–4 minutes until golden brown, then remove with a slotted spoon or frying spider and place on a plate lined with kitchen paper.

3. Keeping the wok of oil on a medium-high heat, fry the Thai basil leaves for no longer than 30 seconds until translucent and crisp. Just take care as the basil leaves are likely to spit in the oil. Scatter the fried leaves and a generous pinch or two of the seasoning over the fried chicken, then toss through and serve.

SALT & SICHUAN PEPPER PRAWNS

PREP: 20 MINS | COOK: 11 MINS | SERVES 2

300g (10½oz) shell-on raw
   tiger prawns
2 tablespoons cornflour
vegetable oil
6–8 garlic cloves, finely chopped
½ thumb-sized piece of ginger,
   peeled and finely chopped
1 large red chilli, finely chopped
1–2 spring onions, finely chopped

SPICE MIX
1 tablespoon Sichuan peppercorns
1 teaspoon salt
½ teaspoon white pepper
pinch of sugar

I once spent a day in Hong Kong watching six chefs from around the world battle it out to win the 'Young Chinese Chef of the Year' award. The speed with which one of the chefs butterflied, deveined and cleaned his prawns with just one swift movement of his cleaver left my mouth wide open. The dish he made, however, is simple. Give it a try!

1. Butterfly the prawns by cutting through the shells down the backs, running your knife through the meat to open them out. Stop slicing just before the tail to keep it intact. Scrape out the black digestive cord, then place the butterflied prawns in a mixing bowl and wash well in cold water. Score horizontally across the prawn meat 4–5 times so that they open up nicely while cooking, then dust them with the cornflour.

2. For the spice mix, toast the Sichuan peppercorns in a dry pan, swirling them around on a medium heat for 1–2 minutes until they pop and become fragrant. Add the salt to the pan, then transfer to a pestle and mortar or spice grinder, add the white pepper and sugar and pound or grind to a powder.

3. Heat 2–3 tablespoons of oil in a frying pan and bring to a high heat. Place the prawns meat-side down in the pan and fry for 3–4 minutes, until they start to turn pink. Turn and cook the prawns until pink all over, then remove from the pan.

4. **Build Your Wok Clock:** Start at 12 o'clock with the garlic, then the ginger, red chilli and spring onions, the spice mix and lastly the fried prawns.

5. Heat 1–2 tablespoons of oil in your wok over a medium heat. Add the garlic, moving it constantly until it starts to brown and separates a little – about 30 seconds. Then add the ginger, chilli and spring onions. Throw in the spice mix and immediately add the cooked prawns to the wok. Toss through 5–6 times in the wok to fully coat the prawns before serving.

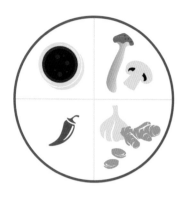

HUNAN TOFU WITH A MEDLEY OF MUSHROOMS

PREP: 7 MINS | COOK: 25 MINS | SERVES 2

350g (12oz) silken tofu, cut into
    1cm (½ inch) thick slices
200g (7oz) mixed mushrooms,
    torn into bite-sized pieces
½ thumb-sized piece of ginger,
    peeled and finely chopped
2 garlic cloves, finely chopped
3 tablespoons Chinese salted
    red chillies (*duo jiao*)
    (swapsies: see below)
vegetable oil
finely sliced spring onions,
    to garnish (optional)

SAUCE
1 tablespoon light soy sauce
¼ teaspoon sugar
100ml (3½fl oz) hot water

Certain ingredients in Chinese cooking are seen as essential for specific regional dishes - like the salted red chillies in this dish. However, the beauty of our cuisine is in its adaptability. If you can't get your hands on this ingredient, roasted red peppers mixed with fried red chillies is a great alternative (see below).

1. Mix the sauce ingredients together in a small bowl. Place the tofu in a large shallow heatproof bowl and steam for 10 minutes in a steamer or an additional wok (see page 20).

2. **Build Your Wok Clock:** Start at 12 o'clock with the mushrooms, followed by the ginger and garlic, the salted red chillies and lastly the sauce.

3. Heat 1 tablespoon of vegetable oil in your wok to a high heat and sear the torn mushrooms for 2 minutes or until golden, then flip and sear again on the other side. Once cooked, carefully remove the lid of the steamer and pour the mushrooms over the top of the tofu, then cover with a lid again to continue steaming.

4. Return the wok to the hob, heat an additional tablespoon of oil on a medium heat and add the ginger and garlic. Stir-fry for 1–2 minutes and then add the salted red chillies and continue to stir-fry for 2–3 minutes before adding the sauce to the wok. Bring to a boil for 3–4 minutes and then switch off the heat.

5. Remove the bowl of tofu from the steamer and pour the sauce over the top of the tofu and mushrooms. Garnish with plenty of sliced spring onions, if liked, and serve.

Salted red chilli alternative: Finely chop 4 large fresh red chillies and 1 roasted red pepper from a jar. Heat 1 tablespoon of vegetable oil to a medium-low heat in a wok, add the chillies, red pepper and ½ teaspoon of salt and fry for 8–10 minutes, stirring well, until softened.

SERIOUSLY SPICY CHICKEN

PREP: 15 MINS, PLUS SOAKING | COOK: 7 MINS | SERVES 2

a generous handful of large
    dried red chillies
1–2 teaspoons Sichuan
    peppercorns
4 skinless, boneless chicken
    thighs, cut into 1cm
    (½ inch) dice
½ thumb-sized piece of ginger,
    peeled and roughly chopped
4 garlic cloves, roughly chopped
1 spring onion, cut into 2cm
    (¾ inch) pieces
3 tablespoons pickled mustard
    greens (za chai), finely diced
    (swapsies: 2 gherkins)
vegetable oil

MARINADE
½ tablespoon chilli powder
    or ground chilli flakes
¼ teaspoon salt
¼ teaspoon sugar
¼ teaspoon white pepper
1 tablespoon Shaoxing rice wine
    (swapsies: dry sherry)
1 teaspoon sesame oil
2 tablespoons cornflour

SAUCE
1 teaspoon Sichuanese chilli
    oil or Chiu Chow chilli oil
    (the paste part)
1 tablespoon light soy sauce
½ teaspoon sugar

I was always told not to play with my food, but this dish was made to be played with! Some restaurants call this 'Chicken swimming in chillies' as there are so many chunks of dried chilli in this dish that you have to search for the pieces of chicken to go with your rice.

1. Soak the dried red chillies in hot water for 10 minutes, then drain and chop into 1–2cm (½–¾ inch) chunks. Grind the Sichuan peppercorns using a pestle and mortar or spice grinder.

2. Place the chicken in a mixing bowl and massage the marinade ingredients into the meat, taking care to add in the cornflour at the very end and mix well. Mix the sauce ingredients together in a small bowl.

3. **Build Your Wok Clock:** Start at 12 o'clock with your marinated chicken, followed by the ginger, garlic and spring onion, pickled mustard greens or gherkins, the ground Sichuan peppercorns, soaked red chillies and lastly the bowl of sauce.

4. Heat 2 tablespoons of vegetable oil in a wok over a high heat until smoking hot. Once smoking hot, add the chicken and sear well for 1–2 minutes until crisp around the edges, turn the chicken pieces over and sear the other side for a further 1–2 minutes. Transfer the chicken to a plate.

5. Place the wok back on a high heat, add ½ tablespoon of vegetable oil and heat to a smoking point, then add the ginger, garlic and spring onion and stir-fry for 30 seconds or so. Then add the pickled mustard greens, followed by the ground Sichuan peppercorns and soaked red chillies, stir-frying for 30 seconds between each addition. Return the chicken to the wok and fold through. Allow it to smoke for 10 seconds, then pour the sauce over the top and stir-fry until the sauce has thickened and coated each piece of chicken. Serve immediately.

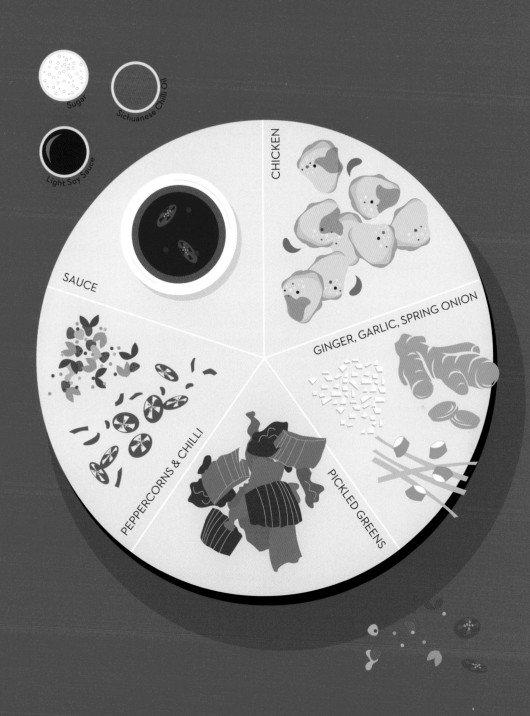

Sugar

Sichuanese Chilli Oil

Light Soy Sauce

SAUCE

CHICKEN

GINGER, GARLIC, SPRING ONION

PICKLED GREENS

PEPPERCORNS & CHILLI

SICHUAN BOILED BEEF

PREP: 15 MINS | COOK: 9 MINS | SERVES 2

300g (10½oz) rib-eye or sirloin
  steak, finely sliced against
  the grain
200g (7oz) beansprouts, rinsed
4 spring onions, finely sliced
1 thumb-sized piece of ginger,
  peeled and finely chopped
3 garlic cloves, finely chopped
2 tablespoons chilli bean sauce
  (*toban jiang*)
1 tablespoon light soy sauce
1 tablespoon Shaoxing rice wine
  (swapsies: dry sherry)
300ml (½ pint) chicken stock
vegetable oil
handful of coriander leaves,
  to garnish

PEPPERCORN PASTE

2 tablespoons vegetable oil
1 tablespoon Sichuan peppercorns
12 dried red chillies

MARINADE

2 teaspoons Shaoxing rice wine
  (swapsies: dry sherry)
½ teaspoon salt
½ tablespoon cornflour

This recipe is something I would usually eat as a treat, so use a good-quality steak and don't skimp on the ingredients – it's worth it! The searing of chilli oil over the top adds to the melt-in-the-mouth finish that makes this so delectable.

1. For the peppercorn paste, heat the oil in a wok at medium-low heat. Fry the Sichuan peppercorns for no more than 30 seconds, then remove from the wok using a slotted spoon. Do the same with the dried red chillies until fragrant (30–60 seconds) then transfer to a sieve over a bowl to catch the excess oil (reserve this). Crush the chillies and peppercorns together into a coarse paste using a pestle and mortar or spice grinder.

2. Give the sliced steak a good bash with the side of your cleaver or knife to flatten and tenderize the meat. Place it in a mixing bowl and massage in the marinade ingredients.

3. **Build Your Wok Clock:** Start at 12 o'clock with the beansprouts followed by the spring onions, ginger and garlic, then the chilli bean sauce, the light soy sauce, rice wine, chicken stock and finally the bowl of marinated sliced beef.

4. Heat ½ teaspoon of vegetable oil in a wok over medium heat. Add the beansprouts and stir-fry for 1 minute until slightly softened and translucent. Transfer to a serving bowl.

5. Add another 1–2 tablespoons of vegetable oil to the wok over medium-high heat and add the spring onions, ginger and garlic and stir-fry for 1–2 minutes until softened and very fragrant. Then add the chilli bean sauce, soy sauce and Shaoxing rice wine, stir-frying for 30 seconds between each ingredient. Next pour the chicken stock in, bring to the boil and simmer for 2–3 minutes.

6. Add the steak slices to the wok and boil for 30–60 seconds. Arrange the meat over the beansprouts in the serving bowl and then pour the rest of the sauce over the top. Scatter the peppercorn paste over the top of the beef. Lastly, heat the reserved chilli-infused oil over a high heat until smoking-hot and pour on top of the paste to sizzle. Garnish with coriander leaves and enjoy.

SWEET & SOUR 'SQUIRREL' FISH

PREP: 7 MINS | COOK: 12 MINS | SERVES 2-4

2 x 300g (10½oz) cod fillets
    with skin
300g (10½oz) cornflour,
    seasoned with 1 teaspoon salt
    and 1 teaspoon pepper
vegetable oil

SAUCE
6 tablespoons tomato ketchup
2 tablespoons light soy sauce
1 tablespoon dark soy sauce
3 tablespoons rice vinegar
3 tablespoons sugar

The names of Chinese recipes are often quite literal. This one, however, is named for its resemblance to a squirrel rather than the thing itself. Although, as my four-year-old son quite rightly pointed out, the fish fillets look more like a hedgehog than a squirrel. The beauty of cutting the fish this way that is that once it is deep fried, the flesh can be simply picked off one piece at a time – perfect for sharing.

1. Lay one of the fish fillets on a board flesh side up and gently score 4–5 times along the length of the flesh, taking care not to break through the skin to keep the fillet intact. Next, turn the fillet horizontally and score the flesh diagonally 8–10 times along the width of the fillet. The end result should look much like an angled grid. Repeat with the other fillet.

2. Place the seasoned cornflour on a large plate. Press the scored fillets flesh side down into the cornflour, then flip and repeat. Take care to make sure the sides of each scored piece of flesh are covered with the cornflour and you can see the lines clearly. The fish should be dry and dusty white all over.

3. Mix the sauce ingredients together in a bowl ready to cook.

4. Deep-fry the coated fish fillets in vegetable oil at 180°C (350°F) (see page 21), lowering them into the oil flesh side down and holding them down with a slotted spoon or tongs to seal all over for about 1 minute. Reduce the heat to medium and continue to deep-fry for 4–5 minutes before turning the fish over for a further 3–4 minutes. Transfer the fish to a plate lined with kitchen paper to drain, before placing on a serving plate.

5. If using a wok, carefully pour out the oil into a heatproof bowl to cool and give your wok a quick wipe with kitchen paper. Place the wok back on the hob and bring ½ tablespoon of vegetable oil to a high heat. Pour the sauce into the wok and bring to a vigorous boil. Once bubbling rapidly, stir once or twice and then pour over the deep-fried fish to finish.

GUANGXI-STYLE STEAMED CHICKEN

PREP: 10 MINS, PLUS MARINATING | COOK: 25-30 MINS | SERVES 2

2 whole chicken legs
    (thigh and drumstick),
    with skin and bone
steamed rice, to serve

MARINADE
2 tablespoons Shaoxing rice
    wine (swapsies: dry sherry)
1/2 teaspoon salt
2 spring onions,
    roughly chopped

NAM TOPPING
100g (3 1/2 oz) Chinese chives,
    wild garlic, garlic shoots or
    spring onions, finely chopped
1/2 thumb-sized piece of ginger,
    peeled and finely chopped
vegetable oil
3 tablespoons light soy sauce
1 tablespoon sesame oil
2 tablespoons toasted
    sesame seeds

Guangxi province in China sits just north of Vietnam. Its cuisine travels around Southeast Asia with its people, and simple iterations of this dish have become extremely popular in both Malaysia and Singapore over generations of movement and diasporas. The Chinese chive topping, called 'nam' by Malaysian Chinese communities, cries out to be spooned over a bowl of steamed rice, so don't forget to make rice to accompany this dish.

1. Mix the marinade ingredients in a shallow heatproof bowl, add the chicken and massage the marinade around the chicken. Cover and leave to marinate overnight, or carry on to cook it straight away.

2. Steam the bowl of chicken for 25 minutes (see page 20). Check whether the chicken is cooked by piercing the thickest part of the joint with a sharp knife. If the juice runs clear, it is cooked; if not, then continue to steam for a further 5 minutes before checking again.

3. To make the nam, place the chives and ginger in a heatproof bowl. Heat 3-4 tablespoons of oil in a wok or frying pan over a high heat until smoking hot, then pour over the chives and ginger. Pour the light soy sauce, sesame oil and sesame seeds over the top and stir it all together.

4. To serve, I recommend chopping the chicken into bite-sized pieces – I like to chop each leg straight through the bone with my cleaver into 5-6 pieces, but if you don't have a cleaver sharp enough (or don't wish to serve it this way) you can just separate the drumsticks from the thighs. Once you have chopped the chicken to your liking, pour the nam over the top and serve with some steamed rice on the side.

CHINESE OMELETTES

PREP: 5 MINS | COOK: 5 MINS | SERVES 2

200g (7oz) green beans,
    trimmed and finely chopped
vegetable oil
1 spring onion, sliced into
    rough chunks

EGG MIXTURE
6 eggs
1½ tablespoons light soy sauce
1 teaspoon sesame oil

Eggs are a wok's best friend and worst enemy. As wok cookery is so fast and fierce, eggs can easily burn. But by mastering the way to cook egg-fried rice or a Chinese omelette in a wok, you will set yourself up for a lifetime of skill enjoyment. Get your *wok hei* right and master the art of your 'wok's air' (see page 18) and that frying pan may just get pushed further and further to the back of your cupboard.

1. Blanch the chopped green beans in a saucepan of boiling water for 30 seconds. Drain through a sieve over the sink and run them under cold water to stop them from cooking any further. Beat the egg mixture ingredients together in a jug or bowl.

2. **Build Your Wok Clock:** Start at 12 o'clock with the egg mixture, followed by the green beans and the spring onion.

3. Heat 2 tablespoons of vegetable oil in a wok on a high heat until the oil is smoking hot, then reduce the heat to medium. Pour half the egg mixture into the wok and allow it to bubble before pushing into the egg with your spatula and giving it a good stir. Pour half the blanched green beans into the egg along with half the chopped spring onion. Allow the egg to bubble up a little again and then fold each side of the omelette over itself in thirds, like folding paper to fit into an envelope, closing up the omelette and keeping the inside of the egg nice and moist. Flip the omelette over to seal fully, then carefully slide onto a plate without breaking it.

4. Now repeat the process again with the remaining ingredients to make a second omelette, and serve.

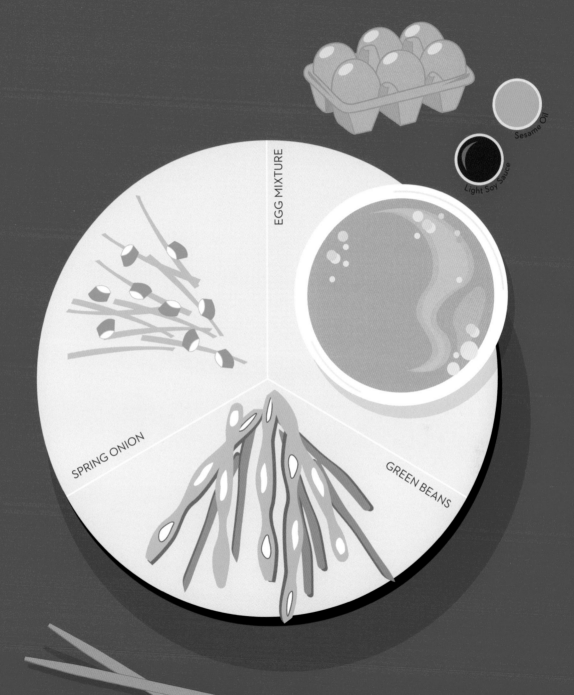

EGG MIXTURE

SPRING ONION

GREEN BEANS

Sesame Oil

Light Soy Sauce

THAI

Contrary to what some may believe, Thai food is not just about the chillies. The cuisine is built by combining a range of herbs and spices (and yes, chillies!) into vibrant blends and colourful pastes. If you've never been, let me paint a picture of what it's like to walk through a typical Bangkok market: vast quantities of fresh fish and seafood laid out on display over ice and newly butchered or cured and dried meats hanging like bunting across many of the stalls. But the first thing you notice is the smell that hits your nose, even before you've stepped into the market itself – the sweet aroma of gingers and galangal, young lemon grass, lime leaves and freshly cracked coconuts with every last spoonful of flesh being squeezed for its milk. Add on top the array of ripening tropical fruits, enriching the sweetness of the humid air. It's these base herbs, natural fruits and coconut sugars that form the basis of the whole cuisine.

I've always been mesmerized by the stark contrast of colour from one curry to another and the unique sweet and sour flavours of Thai stir-fries. Although these dishes are often cooked in a wok, in Thailand there seems to be a slightly slower pace and rhythm to wok cooking. Curries are cooked out for longer to intensify the flavour of the sauce, and noodles are often lightly braised or boiled in a wok for a few minutes longer than in a classic Chinese chow mein.

The intensity of the pounded pastes and the strong, sweet, sour and salty sauces are the driving force and foundation behind many Thai recipes. They are cooked using simple frying pans, woks, grills and, of course, the king and queen of the Thai kitchen: the gigantic pestle and mortar. If you are going to cook a lot of Thai food,

I highly recommend investing in a large, hefty pestle and mortar for best results. These large pounding implements are key to bringing out the essential oils of all the core ingredients used to make these unique and flavourful pastes, and help to pound even more flavour into simple toppings for some of the most addictive, satisfying dishes like Larb in Lettuce (see page 78).

I'd go as far to say that when organizing your kitchen for cooking good Thai food at home, turn your attention to making some room for ingredients in your fridge and freezer rather than in the kitchen cupboard. Start with simpler, easy-to-find aromatics such as garlic and ginger, then move on to the sweeter cousins like Thai shallots (which I have replaced with red onions or shallots in this book to make things easier), galangal, then ginger, lemon grass, lime leaves, tamarind concentrates and lime juice for natural sour flavours. Many of these Thai ingredients are more mellow and citrusy than the aromatic base spices that we find in Western supermarkets (galangal versus ginger is a great example), but the recipes will still be delicious using easy-to-find alternatives. Cook with what you have access to! Most Thai dishes are topped off or seasoned with fish sauce for saltiness and palm sugar for balance. I find that using good-quality coconut milk or coconut water adds a natural sweetness to many dishes without the need for too much additional sugar.

When cooking these Thai recipes, I recommend you use the suggested quantities of chillies, fish sauce and palm sugar as a guide rather than gospel. Once confident with the cooking techniques, feel free to change quantities as you see fit to find your own preferred balance of sweet, sour, salty, spicy and savoury flavours.

THAI CURRY PASTES

PREP: 15 MINS EACH | MAKES 5–6 PORTIONS

RED CURRY PASTE

5 large fresh red chillies
5 dried red chillies, soaked
    in hot water for 10 minutes
1 red onion
2 garlic cloves
½ thumb-sized piece of
    galangal or ginger
2 lemon grass stalks, trimmed
4 lime leaves
1 teaspoon ground turmeric
1 teaspoon shrimp paste
    or 2 tablespoons crispy
    fried shallots
small handful of coriander
    stalks and leaves
1 teaspoon ground cumin
1 teaspoon coriander seeds
1 tablespoon paprika

GREEN CURRY PASTE

6 green chillies
½ red onion
1 garlic clove
½ thumb-sized piece of
    galangal or ginger
1 lemon grass stalk, trimmed
2 lime leaves
large handful of chopped
    coriander stalks
1 teaspoon ground turmeric
½ teaspoon shrimp paste
    or 2 tablespoons crispy
    fried shallots

YELLOW CURRY PASTE

1 red birds' eye chilli
1½ red onions
3 garlic cloves
1 thumb-sized piece of
    galangal or ginger
2 teaspoons ground turmeric
1 tablespoon crispy fried shallots

When it comes to Thai cookery, a large pestle and mortar is your best friend – bashing a curry paste brings out all the essential flavourful oils from the herbs and spices. Curry pastes can be used to make numerous dishes. Here are three colourful and flavourful pastes to help you build up the base flavour of the next few dishes.

1. Always start by peeling and finely chopping the base ingredients such as chillies, onion, garlic, galangal or ginger, lemon grass and lime leaves. Place them into a large mortar along with the rest of the ingredients for the paste you are making and pound them together into a smooth paste. This may take 10–15 minutes of good pounding. You could also use a food processor to do this, but if you do I would recommend adding 1–2 tablespoons of vegetable oil to help the machine make a smoother paste.

2. All these curry pastes can be frozen. The easiest way to do this is to freeze in ice cube trays or in a thin layer on a tray, so the pastes can easily be portioned and defrosted to use for different recipes as and when needed.

GREEN CHICKEN CURRY

PREP: 10 MINS | COOK: 40 MINS | SERVES 2

3-4 tablespoons Green Curry Paste (see page 66)
200g (7oz) skinless, boneless chicken thighs, roughly diced
400ml (14fl oz) can of coconut milk
2 lime leaves
3-4 Thai aubergines, halved, or 1 small aubergine, cut into chunks
4-5 baby sweetcorn, halved lengthways
50g (2oz) sugarsnaps
3 tablespoons fish sauce, or to taste
1 tablespoon palm sugar (swapsies: soft brown sugar), or to taste
vegetable oil

TO GARNISH
small handful of Thai basil leaves
sliced red chilli

The trick to a good Thai curry is both a lovely homemade paste and gradually adding the coconut milk to build a depth of flavour. You could use this recipe to make red and yellow curries too, just by swapping out the paste.

1. **Build Your Wok Clock:** Start at 12 o'clock with the green curry paste, followed by the chicken pieces, the coconut milk, the lime leaves, aubergine, baby sweetcorn, sugarsnaps and lastly the fish sauce and palm sugar.

2. Heat 1–2 tablespoons of vegetable oil in your wok over a medium-low heat then add the curry paste. Stir-fry the paste for 4–5 minutes until fragrant and aromatic. Now add the chicken and fold into the paste while continuing to stir-fry for 2–3 minutes. Next, pour 4–5 tablespoons of the coconut milk over the chicken and stir well, scraping the wok to deglaze any paste that has stuck to the bottom.

3. Bring to a boil, then pour in half the remaining coconut milk. Bring to a boil once more, give the curry a stir and then pour the remaining coconut milk in the wok. Return to a boil then add the lime leaves and aubergine, reduce the heat and simmer for 20 minutes.

4. Add the baby sweetcorn and simmer for another 3 minutes, then add the sugarsnaps and cook for a further 2–3 minutes. Season to your preferred taste with fish sauce and sugar, using the quantities above as guidance. Serve scattered with Thai basil and red chillies.

GREEN CURRY PASTE

FISH SAUCE & SUGAR

CHICKEN

SUGARSNAPS & SWEETCORN

LIME LEAVES & AUBERGINE

COCONUT MILK

PAD THAI

PREP: 15–20 MINS, PLUS SOAKING & DRYING | COOK: 8 MINS | SERVES 2

150g (5½oz) flat rice noodles
2 eggs, lightly beaten
100g (3½oz) firm tofu,
    cut into batons
½ tablespoon Thai chilli paste
    (*nam prik pau*) or Red Curry
    Paste (see page 66)
100g (3½oz) Chinese chives,
    wild garlic or garlic shoots,
    cut into matchsticks
handful of beansprouts, rinsed
12 raw peeled tiger prawns,
    deveined
vegetable oil

SAUCE
2 tablespoons tamarind
    concentrate
2 tablespoons fish sauce
2 tablespoons lime juice
3 teaspoons palm sugar
    (swapsies: soft brown sugar)
2 tablespoons kecap manis
    (sweet soy sauce)

TO GARNISH
25g (1oz) roasted peanuts,
    roughly chopped
1 lime, cut into wedges
handful of coriander leaves
1–2 teaspoons chilli flakes
    (optional)

An introduction to Thai cuisine isn't complete without a recipe for Pad Thai. It's a relatively modern recipe which was born out of the want of a Thai national dish. It's a wonderful way to show off Thai culture, through a plate of good, wholesome, tasty rice noodles.

1. Soak the noodles in hot water for 5–6 minutes until tender, then drain and refresh in cold water. Drain again and spread out on a clean tea towel to dry for 10 minutes. Then mix the sauce ingredients together in a small bowl until the sugar fully dissolves.

2. **Build Your Wok Clock:** Start at 12 o'clock with the beaten egg, followed by the tofu, Thai chilli paste, Chinese chives and beansprouts, prawns, soaked noodles and lastly the sauce.

3. Heat 1–2 tablespoons of vegetable oil in your wok over a high heat then pour in the eggs. Allow the eggs to bubble up, and then start to push into them and fold them as you would if you were cooking an omelette. Once half-cooked, push the eggs to the back of your wok, add 1 tablespoon of vegetable oil to the base of the wok and add the tofu pieces and the Thai chilli paste. Stir-fry the tofu for 2–3 minutes until lightly browned. Add the chives and beansprouts, mix with the egg to combine for 30 seconds, then push to the side of the wok.

4. Add another ½ tablespoon of vegetable oil and bring to a smoking point before adding the prawns. Sear well on each side (about 1 minute) then bring the vegetables back over the top of the prawns. Add the rice noodles, followed immediately by the sauce. Give your wok a vigorous shake while stirring with your ladle or spatula (like a 'tummy and head' movement, see page 19). Stop the movement, allow the sauce to boil and repeat the movement every 30 seconds. This will evenly distribute the sauce throughout the noodles. Continue for 2–3 minutes until the noodles are fully coated and just starting to stick to the wok. Serve garnished with the chopped peanuts, lime wedges, coriander and chilli flakes.

THAI FISHCAKES

PREP: 12 MINS | COOK: 12 MINS | MAKES 20-25

handful of coriander
200g (7oz) skinless white fish
    fillets (such as cod, hake,
    haddock, pollack or sea bass),
    roughly chopped
200g (7oz) raw peeled prawns,
    deveined
2 tablespoons Red Curry Paste
    (see page 66)
1 spring onion, finely chopped
¼ teaspoon salt
¼ teaspoon black pepper
1 tablespoon cornflour
vegetable oil
sweet chilli sauce, to serve

These light and flavourful fishcakes make a wonderful starter or street food-style snack. They also work well on the side of any main dish, such as the Royal Thai Crab Curry & Vermicelli (see page 76).

1. Pick the coriander leaves off the stalks and roughly chop the stalks, keeping leaves and stalks separate.

2. Dab the fish and prawns on kitchen paper to dry, then place in a food processor and pulse into a rough paste. Add the red curry paste and pulse again to combine. Add the coriander stalks and all but a pinch of spring onion and pulse a couple of times. Add the seasoning and cornflour and pulse one last time. Once well combined, transfer the mixture to a bowl. Fry a teaspoon of the mixture in a little vegetable oil until cooked, taste and adjust the seasoning as needed.

3. Divide the mixture into 20-25 ping pong-sized balls and flatten each into a patty, dipping your hands in a bowl of cold water to prevent the mixture sticking.

4. Deep-fry the fishcakes in batches in vegetable oil at 180°C (350°F) for 3-4 minutes until golden brown and rising to the surface (see page 21), carefully adding them one by one to the oil. Transfer the fishcakes to a plate lined with kitchen paper.

5. Serve with sweet chilli sauce, the remaining sliced spring onion and the coriander leaves.

THAI BASIL DUCK

PREP: 15 MINS, PLUS RESTING | COOK: 12 MINS | SERVES 2

2 duck breasts
½ teaspoon salt
1–2 tablespoons Red Curry Paste
  (see page 66)
1 red onion, finely sliced
100g (3½oz) mangetout
large handful of Thai basil leaves
vegetable oil

MARINADE
1 teaspoon palm sugar
  (swapsies: soft brown sugar)
1 tablespoon fish sauce
1 tablespoon sesame oil
¼ teaspoon ground turmeric

SAUCE
50ml (2fl oz) chicken stock
100ml (3½fl oz) coconut water
½ tablespoon fish sauce

TO GARNISH
Thai basil leaves

Triple-cooking your duck breasts may seem a little faffy, but trust me when I say it's well worth the effort.

1. Fill your wok to halfway up the sides with boiling water. Over a high heat, blanch the duck breasts for 2 minutes to remove the fatty impurities, then drain through a sieve. This step will help your duck to crisp up when cooked. Give your wok a quick clean and dry and then place back on the hob.

2. Pat the duck breasts dry with a piece of kitchen paper then rub the salt over the skin. Place the duck breasts skin-side down in the wok over a low heat and slowly bring up to a medium heat to draw out the oil from the skin. Once on medium, sear the duck skin-side down for 4–5 minutes until the skin is crispy and golden brown, then turn over to sear the other side for 1 minute.

3. Transfer the duck to a plate and allow to rest for 5 minutes. Once cooled, cut the duck into 2–3mm (⅛ inch) thick slices, leaving a sliver of salty skin on each slice. Place in a mixing bowl and massage the marinade ingredients into the duck and set aside ready to stir-fry.

4. Mix the sauce ingredients together in a small bowl.

5. **Build Your Wok Clock:** Start at 12 o'clock with the red curry paste, followed by the red onion and mangetout, the marinated duck, the sauce and lastly the Thai basil.

6. Heat 1 tablespoon of vegetable oil in a wok over a medium heat. Add the red curry paste and stir-fry for 1–2 minutes until it becomes fragrant but not browned. Add the red onion and mangetout and stir-fry for a further minute. Bring the wok to a high heat. Once the paste starts to brown slightly, add the duck and leave for 30 seconds without moving. Now pour the sauce over the duck and bring to a vigorous boil for 1 minute before switching off the heat. Add a generous handful of Thai basil leaves, folding them into the stir-fry. Serve garnished with more Thai basil leaves.

ROYAL THAI CRAB CURRY & VERMICELLI

PREP: 10 MINS | COOK: 35 MINS | SERVES 2

3 tablespoons Yellow Curry
   Paste (see page 66)
2 lemon grass stalks,
   trimmed and bruised
6 lime leaves
100g (3½oz) brown crab meat
   (optional)
100ml (3½fl oz) coconut milk
200ml (7fl oz) chicken or
   vegetable stock
300ml (½ pint) coconut water
1 crab head shell (saved from
   the dressed crab, see below)
1–2 tablespoons fish sauce,
   or to taste
1–2 teaspoons palm sugar
   (swapsies: soft brown sugar),
   or to taste
200–300g (7–10½oz) freshly
   picked white crab meat
   from a dressed crab
vegetable oil

TO SERVE
50–100g (1¾–3½oz) dried
   rice vermicelli
2 soft-boiled eggs at
   room temperature,
   peeled and halved
3 baby cucumbers or
   ½ cucumber, sliced
3–4 Little Gem lettuce leaves
handful of Thai basil leaves

Yung Siam is a quirky and memorable restaurant we stumbled across while exploring the old city of Bangkok. It felt like dining in an old colonel's living room. The food was perfectly balanced: not too sweet, not too salty, just the right level of spice. The yellow crab curry that I'm trying to recreate here is something of a phenomenon and requires a bit of nuance: a far cry from most British takeaway curries, delicious as they may be.

1. Boil the rice vermicelli in a saucepan of water for 3–4 minutes until tender, then drain and cool in a bowl of cold water. Drain again and twist into neat little nests around a fork, then arrange on a large serving plate with the egg halves, cucumber, lettuce and Thai basil.

2. **Build Your Wok Clock:** Start at 12 o'clock with the yellow curry paste, followed by the lemon grass and lime leaves, brown crab meat (if using), coconut milk, chicken stock and coconut water, the crab head shell, fish sauce, palm sugar and picked white crab meat.

3. Bring 1–2 tablespoons of vegetable oil to a medium heat in your wok and gently fry the curry paste for 3–5 minutes or until fragrant. Once the aroma changes from grassy to sweet and aromatic, add the lemon grass, lime leaves and any brown crab meat, if using, then pour in the coconut milk and bring to the boil. Boil for 2–3 minutes, then add the chicken stock and coconut water and bring to the boil once more. Now add the crab head shell and reduce the heat to simmer for 10 minutes.

4. Remove the crab shell then season with fish sauce and sugar. Taste for a balance of sweet and savoury flavours and adjust as necessary. Lastly, add the white crab meat, simmer for 2–3 minutes and serve with the plate of eggs and vegetables to complement the curry.

LARB IN LETTUCE

PREP: 15 MINS | COOK: 11 MINS | SERVES 2

handful of dry rice grains
300g (10½oz) minced pork
    or chicken
3 garlic cloves, finely chopped
1 red onion, finely sliced
small handful of
    coriander leaves
small handful of mint leaves
handful of Thai basil leaves
    (optional)
vegetable oil
sliced spring onion, to garnish
½ head of Romaine lettuce,
    leaves separated, to serve

MARINADE
1 tablespoon chilli flakes
½ tablespoon light soy sauce

SAUCE
1 tablespoon fish sauce
juice of 1 lime
½ teaspoon sugar

Larb or *laab* is a popular warm meat salad that usually sits next to a *som tam* (papaya salad) and some sticky Thai rice. It's spicy, sour, packed full of fresh herbs and a great way to use up leftover ingredients. The minced pork can easily be swapped out for any type of minced protein.

1. Toast the rice grains in a dry wok on a medium heat for 4–5 minutes until uniformly golden brown. Allow to cool, then grind the grains to a powder using a pestle and mortar or spice grinder. Return the wok to a medium heat and toast the chilli flakes for the marinade for 30 seconds or so until aromatic. Crush the chilli flakes to a powder using a pestle and mortar or spice grinder.

2. Massage the marinade ingredients into the minced meat and set aside. Mix the sauce ingredients in a small bowl.

3. **Build Your Wok Clock:** Start at 12 o'clock with the marinated meat, followed by the garlic, red onion, the sauce, then finally the herb leaves.

4. Heat 1 tablespoon of vegetable oil in a wok over a high heat then add the marinated minced meat. Stir-fry to sear for 2–3 minutes, then add the garlic and stir-fry for another minute. Next add the red onion and fry for a further 30–60 seconds until fragrant before pouring the sauce into the wok. Allow the sauce to boil for up to 1 minute, then switch off the hob. Scatter the herbs over the mixture and fold through. Sprinkle with toasted rice powder and spring onion and serve with the lettuce leaves on the side.

MINCED MEAT

GARLIC

RED ONION

SAUCE

Lime Juice

Sugar

Fish Sauce

FISH SAUCE WINGS

PREP: 20 MINS | COOK: 15 MINS | SERVES 2

8 chicken wings, sliced through
    to separate the flats and
    the drums
vegetable oil
8 garlic cloves, finely sliced
    (swapsies: 5–6 tablespoons
    ready-fried garlic)
2 birds' eye chillies, finely sliced
1 spring onion, finely sliced
½ red onion, finely sliced

MARINADE
2 tablespoons fish sauce
½ teaspoon ground cumin
½ teaspoon baking powder
6–7 tablespoons cornflour

SAUCE
2 tablespoons palm sugar
    (swapsies: soft brown sugar)
3 tablespoons fish sauce
juice of ½ lime
3–4 tablespoons hot water

In my family, chicken wings can be eaten any time of day. They are the perfect snack, lunch, dinner, or even beachside brunch. This dish tastes like a holiday on a plate; have a coconut or cocktail ready, imagine the palm trees and get ready to tuck in! To save time, try using ready-made crispy fried garlic, available in most Asian supermarkets.

1. Place the chicken pieces in a large mixing bowl and massage the marinade ingredients well into the meat, adding the cornflour at the end.

2. For the crispy fried garlic, heat 6–7 tablespoons of vegetable oil in a wok or saucepan over a low heat and fry the sliced garlic, stirring constantly, until golden brown. Drain through a sieve over a bowl to catch the oil, then tip the garlic onto a sheet of kitchen paper to drain off the excess oil.

3. Mix the sauce ingredients together in a small bowl until the sugar fully dissolves. Set aside a few slices of chilli and a pinch of spring onion for garnish.

4. **Build Your Wok Clock:** Start at 12 o'clock with the bowl of marinated chicken wings, followed by the red onion and spring onion, the chillies and lastly the sauce.

5. Deep-fry the chicken wings in vegetable oil at 170°C (340°F) for 1 minute (see page 21), then reduce the heat to medium-low. Continue to deep-fry for 6–8 minutes, turning the chicken wings occasionally until very crisp and golden brown. Transfer the chicken to a plate lined with kitchen paper.

6. If using your wok for deep-frying, carefully pour out the oil into a heatproof bowl and wipe the wok with kitchen paper. Place the wok back over a medium heat, add 1 tablespoon of oil and stir-fry the red onion and spring onion for 1–2 minutes. Add the chillies, increase the heat to high and pour in the sauce. Bring to a boil for 1–2 minutes until reduced by half and a light syrupy texture. Add the fried chicken into the wok and fold through until fully coated. Scatter with the crispy fried garlic and reserved spring onion and chilli and serve.

1 litre (1¾ pints) chicken stock
2 tablespoons Thai chilli paste
  (*nam prik pao*) or Red Curry
  Paste (see page 66)
125ml (4fl oz) evaporated milk
3 tablespoons fish sauce
150g (5½oz) chestnut
  mushrooms, halved
150g (5½oz) oyster mushrooms,
  roughly torn into chunks
8 shell-on raw tiger prawns,
  peeled and deveined
  (heads and shells reserved)
juice of 1 lime
vegetable oil

BASE INGREDIENTS
heads and shells from the
  prawns (see above)
1 thumb-sized piece of ginger,
  peeled and sliced
1 thumb-sized piece of galangal,
  peeled and sliced (optional)
2 lemon grass stalks, trimmed,
  bruised and sliced
1-2 red birds' eye chillies,
  pierced with the tip
  of your knife
6 lime leaves, roughly torn

GARNISH
finely sliced red chilli
handful of coriander leaves
1 lime, cut into wedges

TOM YUM KUNG

PREP: 15 MINS | COOK: 30 MINS | SERVES 2

The first time I had *tom yum kung* in Thailand, it was so packed full of chilli, I took one sip and couldn't taste anything for the rest of the meal. I learned there and then that hot and sour soup made with a base flavour of citrussy herbs (rather than just heat), with a chilli layer on top, provides a more addictive level of pleasure-pain that makes you want more and more, rather than just blowing out your taste buds with heat.

1. **Build Your Wok Clock:** Start at 12 o'clock with the prawn heads and shells, followed by the ginger and galangal (if using), lemon grass, pierced birds' eye chillies, lime leaves, chicken stock, Thai chilli paste, evaporated milk, fish sauce, mushrooms, prawns and finally the lime juice.

2. Heat 1 tablespoon of vegetable oil in your wok over a high heat. Add in the prawn heads and shells and fry until pink (about 1-2 minutes). Now add the ginger and galangal (if using), followed by the lemon grass, chillies and lime leaves, and give it all a good stir. Let the fragrant mixture cook for 3-4 minutes before pouring in the chicken stock and giving the base of the wok a scrape with a spoon or spatula. Bring to the boil.

3. Next add the chilli paste and give the soup a stir. Reduce the heat down to low and simmer for 15-20 minutes, skimming any scum off the top of the soup using a ladle or spoon about halfway through the cooking time. It helps to dip the spoon in cold water between skims if there is a lot of scum.

4. Remove the prawn heads and shells from the wok along with any large chunks of ginger, galangal, lemon grass and chillies using a slotted spoon. While still over a low heat, pour in the evaporated milk followed by the fish sauce. Add the mushrooms and prawns and continue to boil for 5 minutes before adding the lime juice. Serve garnished with chilli, coriander and lime wedges.

STEAMED FISH WITH LEMON GRASS & LIME BROTH

PREP: 10 MINS | COOK: 14 MINS | SERVES 2

300g (10½oz) whole
    sea bass, or 2 sea bass
    or sea bream fillets
5 lemon grass stalks,
    trimmed and bruised
1 thumb-sized piece of
    galangal or ginger,
    peeled and finely sliced
handful of coriander, leaves
    and stalks separated
vegetable oil

LIME BROTH
3 birds' eye chillies, pierced
    with the tip of your knife
8 garlic cloves, roughly sliced
200ml (7fl oz) chicken stock
2 teaspoons palm sugar
    (swapsies: soft brown sugar)
2 tablespoons fish sauce
juice of 2 limes

Steaming fish is the best way to maintain its delicate texture. This Thai recipe uses strong and zingy flavours to both accentuate and balance the natural sweetness of the fish and is complemented by the garlic-enriched broth.

1. Make 3 diagonal slits across the skin of the whole fish on each side. Place the fish in a large shallow heatproof bowl and stuff the cavity with the lemon grass and galangal or ginger. If using fillets, sandwich the aromatics between the 2 fillets with the skin on the outside as if the fish was still whole. Steam the bowl of fish for 12 minutes (see page 20).

2. Meanwhile, to make the lime broth, heat a dry saucepan over a medium heat. Add the chillies and cook for 30-60 seconds, then add the garlic and bring to a high heat. Once hot, add the coriander stalks and immediately pour in the chicken stock, palm sugar and fish sauce and quickly bring to a vigorous boil. Once boiling, reduce the heat to low and simmer for 10 minutes then remove from the heat and pour the lime juice into the stock.

3. To check the whole fish is cooked, gently pull on one of the dorsal fins (the top fin). If it comes away easily, the fish is cooked through. Carefully remove the bowl from the steamer and cover with the wok lid over the work surface to keep hot. Pour out the steaming water then return the wok to the hob over a high heat. Now heat 2 tablespoons of vegetable oil in the wok until smoking hot. Scatter half the coriander leaves on the top of the steamed fish then pour the hot oil over the top of the leaves to sizzle. Pour the lime broth over the top of the fish, garnish with the remaining coriander and serve.

5 large dried red chillies
4 ducks' eggs or 6 hens' eggs
    at room temperature
2 garlic cloves, finely chopped
vegetable oil

SAUCE
3 tablespoons tamarind
    concentrate
2 teaspoons palm sugar
    (swapsies: soft brown sugar)
1½ tablespoons fish sauce
5 tablespoons hot water
½ teaspoon dark soy sauce

TO GARNISH
2 tablespoons ready-made
    crispy fried shallots
¼ teaspoon ground chilli flakes
    or chilli powder
handful of coriander leaves

SON-IN-LAW EGGS

PREP: 5 MINS, PLUS SOAKING | COOK: 12 MINS | SERVES 2

The origin stories of this dish (known in Thailand as *kai look kuey*) are endless and varied. My favourite story is that the dish was made for a son-in-law as a warning from a proper Thai-ger mother-in-law to make sure to look after her daughter properly or else she'd deep-fry his 'eggs'. Take what you wish from this story, but expect good-tasting eggs.

1. Soak the dried red chillies in hot water for 10 minutes, then drain. Mix the sauce ingredients together in a small bowl, stirring until the sugar has dissolved.

2. Bring a saucepan of water to a boil and carefully lay the eggs into the pan. Boil ducks' eggs for 6 minutes or hens' eggs for 5 minutes, then drain off the hot water and cover the eggs in ice-cold water to stop the cooking. After about 5 minutes when the eggs are cool, peel the eggs and pat dry on kitchen paper.

3. **Build Your Wok Clock:** Start at 12 o'clock with the boiled eggs, followed by the garlic, soaked and drained red chillies, and finally the sauce.

4. Deep-fry the eggs in vegetable oil at 180°C (350°F) for 1–2 minutes until golden brown (see page 21). Transfer the eggs to a plate lined with kitchen paper to drain, then cut them in half and place on a serving plate.

5. If using your wok for deep-frying, carefully pour out the oil into a heatproof bowl to cool. Heat the wok to a high heat with the residual oil, add the garlic and stir-fry for 30 seconds before adding the soaked red chillies. Sear the chillies for a further 30 seconds then pour the sauce into the wok and bring to a vigorous boil. Once boiling, continue to cook for 2–3 minutes, then pour the bubbling sauce over the top of the eggs. Garnish with a generous scattering of fried shallots, chilli powder and coriander leaves.

BANGKOK CRAB OMELETTE

PREP: 7 MINS | COOK: 5 MINS | SERVES 2

6 eggs
1 tablespoon fish sauce
1½ tablespoons plain flour
    or rice flour
300g (10½oz) white crab meat
vegetable oil

NUOC CHAM
DIPPING SAUCE

1 garlic clove, finely chopped
1 birds' eye chilli, finely chopped
juice of 1 lime
2 tablespoons fish sauce
1 tablespoon palm sugar
    or honey

This extraordinary omelette has recently been made famous by a Bangkok street food vendor named Jai Fay who was featured in a Netflix series. Her technique involves deep-frying the omelette, all the while carefully moving the egg around and controlling the heat to avoid burning it. It took me three attempts to master the technique and I'm a professional chef, so here's a simpler version to try.

1. Break the eggs into a mixing bowl, add the fish sauce and flour and beat well. Tip the crab meat over the top of the eggs. Mix the dipping sauce ingredients together in a small bowl, stirring until the sugar has dissolved.

2. Heat 5–6 tablespoons of vegetable oil in a wok to a medium heat. Pour the egg mixture through a sieve into the wok and allow it to bubble for 10 seconds, then tip the crabmeat out of the sieve into the middle of the omelette. Turn the heat up high and immediately fold over the sides of the omelette to cover the crabmeat. Turn the omelette over to seal the folds, then reduce the heat to medium-low.

3. Use 2 spatulas to firmly squeeze along the sides of the omelette to create a regular burrito shape. Keep squeezing and shaping the sides for 3–4 minutes until the omelette is firm and golden all over. Transfer the omelette to a plate lined with kitchen paper to drain off any excess oil, then slice into 4 pieces and serve with the dipping sauce.

VIETNAMESE

Much like the millions of motorbikes whizzing through the streets of Ho Chi Minh City each day, Vietnamese cuisine is constantly moving and evolving with each new cultural influence. Vietnamese communities approach this constant movement and evolution within the cuisine with a long-practiced method of flavour building, adding layers and ingredients to create unique flavours reflective of their local produce and circumstances. You can see these one-of-a-kind combinations in recipes such as Turmeric & Dill Fish (see page 98). In traditional French cuisine, dill is finely chopped and mixed with a beurre blanc sauce before being poured over a piece of fried or poached fish. In this Vietnamese dish (which, for me personally, is far superior when it comes to flavour), large handfuls of fresh dill, stalks and all, are flash-fried at the last minute then tucked into a sweet, salty and savoury sauce alongside the subtle fish flavours and earthy turmeric. We could all take a leaf out of the Vietnamese kitchen bible and learn from their approach to food and cooking. Vietnamese cooks look at what's in front of them, grab every learning opportunity with both hands, combine that with their innate passion for fresh produce and leafy herbs, and then marry it all together with their sixth sense of how to perfectly season their food to leave our palates wanting more.

A wok is not the primary tool in a Vietnamese kitchen. At it is influenced as much by both French and Chinese food, frying pans and hot plates are just as prominent. However, as you walk along the street food stalls in Vietnam, you'll notice even dishes like *bánh xèo* (Vietnamese pancakes) are still being made in large, thin metalled woks, even though you would think they would be easier made in a frying pan.

The recipes that I have included in this chapter are all easily doable in a wok. Each is hearty enough to be a main meal with some rice or even just a herby salad on the side.

In fact, I'd say that with most Vietnamese meals, setting up the table with basketfuls of fresh leafy herbs wouldn't go amiss. Every good Vietnamese meal I have ever eaten has come with handfuls of coriander or sawtooth coriander, mint, Thai basil, dill or other fresh leafy herbs. Aside from the fresh herbs, other must-have pantry items are fish sauce, the key seasoning ingredient, and limes and chillies. So when you're cooking any of the dishes from this chapter, make sure you have space in your fridge for the fresh herbs! Vietnamese food just wouldn't be the same without them.

QUICK CHICKEN PHO

PREP: 15 MINS, PLUS SOAKING & DRYING | COOK: 32 MINS | SERVES 2

2 whole chicken legs
  (thighs and drumsticks),
  with skin and bone
2 litres (3½ pints) chicken stock
½ large onion, cut into wedges
1 thumb-sized piece of ginger,
  peeled and finely sliced
1 tablespoon palm sugar
  (swapsies: soft brown sugar),
  or to taste
3-4 tablespoons fish sauce,
  or to taste

BASE SPICES
2 teaspoons coriander seeds
2 cloves
2 black cardamom pods
2 star anise
5-10cm (2-4 inch) piece
  of cinnamon bark

TO SERVE
150g (5½oz) flat rice noodles
handful of beansprouts, rinsed
handful of mint, coriander
  and Thai basil leaves
1 spring onion, finely sliced
2 red chillies, finely sliced
1 lime, cut into wedges

The success of this Vietnamese comfort food lies in a good stock. At School of Wok, we always have chicken stock frozen in large ice trays, or you can buy ready-made stock. Look out for one with as little salt as possible so you can season to taste.

1. Soak the noodles in hot water for 8-10 minutes until tender, then drain and refresh in cold water. Drain again and spread out on a clean tea towel to dry for 10 minutes.

2. Place the chicken legs in a wok over a high heat. Pour boiling water over the chicken until fully covered and bring to a boil for 3-4 minutes to remove any scum. Then pour the water away and rinse the chicken under cold water.

3. **Build Your Wok Clock:** Start at 12 o'clock with the base spices, followed by the chicken stock, blanched chicken legs, onion and ginger, palm sugar, fish sauce, the soaked noodles, and lastly the beansprouts.

4. Heat your wok over a medium heat then add in the base spices. Toast in the dry pan for 1-2 minutes until aromatic, then pour in the chicken stock and bring to a boil. Next add the blanched chicken legs, onion and ginger. Maintaining a medium heat, cover with a lid and boil for 20-25 minutes.

5. Check the chicken legs are cooked, then remove them from the wok. Add the palm sugar and fish sauce to season the broth and taste: if you prefer it to be more salty, then add more fish sauce a tablespoon at a time. If you prefer it a bit sweeter, then add a little more sugar. Remove the skin from the cooked chicken legs and finely shred the meat.

6. Reheat the soaked noodles in the broth for 1 minute, then transfer to a large serving bowl or divide between 2 bowls. Blanch the beansprouts in the broth for 30 seconds, then place on top of the noodles. Add a generous handful of shredded chicken, followed by a generous handful of mixed herbs on the side. Ladle in the chicken broth and garnish with spring onion, sliced chillies and lime wedges.

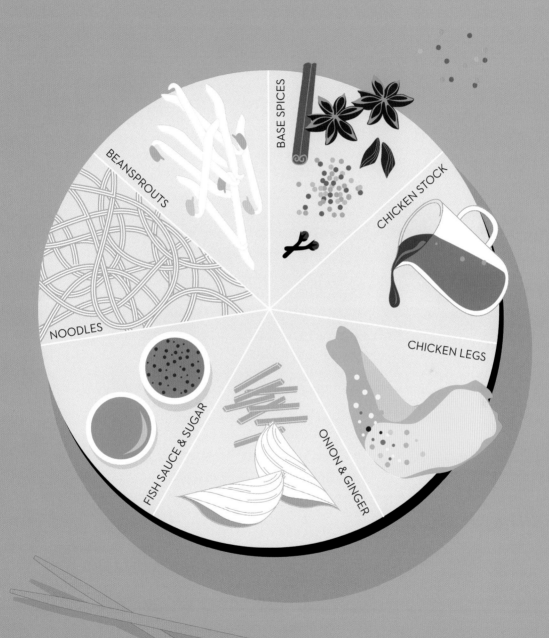

BASE SPICES

CHICKEN STOCK

CHICKEN LEGS

ONION & GINGER

FISH SAUCE & SUGAR

NOODLES

BEANSPROUTS

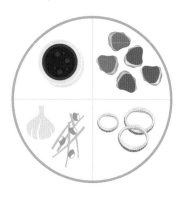

SHAKING BEEF SALAD WITH PICKLED RED ONION

PREP: 20 MINS, PLUS PICKLING | COOK: 5 MINS | SERVES 2

300g (10½oz) rib-eye steak, cut into large dice
150g (5½oz) heritage baby tomatoes or cherry tomatoes, halved
100g (3½oz) watercress, rinsed
2 baby cucumbers, sliced diagonally into wedges
½ red onion, finely sliced
1 spring onion, roughly chopped
2-3 garlic cloves, finely sliced
vegetable oil
handful of coriander and mint leaves, to garnish

PICKLED RED ONION
½ red onion, finely sliced
100g (3½oz) radishes, finely sliced (optional)
6 tablespoons rice vinegar
1 tablespoon sugar
½ tablespoon sea salt

MARINADE
½ teaspoon sea salt flakes
¼ teaspoon cracked black pepper
½ teaspoon sugar
1 teaspoon sesame oil
½ tablespoon cornflour

SAUCE
1½ tablespoons oyster sauce
1 tablespoon fish sauce
½ tablespoon sugar
juice of ½ lime

This dish requires your wok to be smoking hot. I would recommend leaving it on a high heat for at least 30-60 seconds before starting this stir-fry. Get that extractor fan on high, open all your windows and put away any laundry hanging in the kitchen – unless you want your clothes, too, to have a smoky finish.

1. For the pickled red onion, place the onion into a small bowl with the radishes, if using. Add the rest of the pickled onion ingredients to the bowl and give it a stir to dissolve the sugar and salt. Set aside for a minimum of 20 minutes.

2. Place the steak in a mixing bowl and massage the marinade ingredients into the meat, saving the cornflour until last. Mix the sauce ingredients together in a separate bowl.

3. Place the tomatoes in a bowl and stir in 2 tablespoons of the pickling liquid from the pickled red onion. Arrange the watercress over a serving plate and scatter the cucumber and tomatoes around.

4. **Build Your Wok Clock:** Start at 12 o'clock with the marinated beef, followed by the (unpickled) red onion, spring onion and garlic, and lastly the sauce.

5. Heat 2 tablespoons of vegetable oil in your wok over a high heat until smoking hot. Swirl the oil around the wok a little and then add the marinated beef and sear for 1 minute on each side. Next add the sliced red onion to the wok and start to fold through. Add the spring onion and garlic and continue to stir-fry for 1-2 minutes, giving the wok a good shake every 20-30 seconds.

6. Now stop shaking the wok to allow the heat to build until smoking. Then quickly pour in the sauce and bring to a vigorous boil. Fold through once or twice to fully coat the beef and vegetables, then spoon onto the top of your salad. Garnish with the herbs and drained pickled red onion.

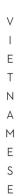

TURMERIC & DILL FISH

PREP: 15 MINS, PLUS SOAKING & DRYING | COOK: 8 MINS | SERVES 2

100g (3½oz) rice vermicelli
400g (14oz) skinless halibut
    or cod fillet, cut into
    bite-sized pieces
8–10 spring onions,
    roughly chopped
large bunch of dill, torn
    into bite-sized pieces
vegetable oil

SAUCE
2 garlic cloves, finely chopped
juice of ½ lime
5 tablespoons water
1 tablespoons fish sauce
1½ tablespoons sugar

MARINADE
½ thumb-sized piece of
    galangal or ginger, peeled
3 garlic cloves
½ small red onion
1 teaspoon ground turmeric
1 tablespoon fish sauce
½ tablespoon cornflour

TO GARNISH
2 tablespoons salted roasted
    peanuts, roughly chopped
small handful of coriander
    leaves
finely sliced spring onion

Traditionally a river fish, similar to catfish, is used for this dish. In Hanoi this dish, called *cha ca la vong* is often grilled first before frying. For ease, I have kept the whole cooking process in a wok, but if you'd rather cook it the traditional way, grill it under a hot grill for 3–4 minutes at the beginning of Step 4, then follow the recipe from there.

1. Soak the vermicelli in hot water for 3–4 minutes until tender, then drain and refresh in cold water. Drain again and spread out on a clean tea towel to dry for 10 minutes. Mix the sauce ingredients together in a small bowl.

2. Blitz the marinade ingredients to a smooth paste in a food processor, or finely chop the ingredients and crush using a pestle and mortar until smooth. Place the fish in a mixing bowl and generously coat it on all sides with the marinade.

3. **Build Your Wok Clock:** Start at 12 o'clock with the marinated fish, followed by the spring onions, dill and lastly the sauce.

4. Heat 2–3 tablespoons of vegetable oil to a high heat in your wok and place the marinated fish in the oil piece by piece, allowing space between each piece of fish so that they can char a little around the edges. Fry in the oil for 2–3 minutes, then use a fish slice to turn the fish and sear the other side. Once the fish is seared well around the edges, reduce the heat to medium, cover the fish pieces with the spring onions and dill and start to fold it all gently into the wok, taking care not to break the pieces of fish. Then pour in the sauce and cook for 1–2 minutes until the herbs have wilted.

5. Garnish the fish with roasted peanuts, coriander leaves and finely sliced spring onion and serve with the noodles on the side.

CRISPY TOFU
IN TOMATO SAUCE

PREP: 10 MINS | COOK: 40 MINS | SERVES 2

vegetable oil
350g (12oz) firm tofu,
    cut into 3cm (1¼ inch)
    cubes or triangles
2 garlic cloves, finely sliced
2 spring onions, green part
    of 1 finely sliced, the rest
    roughly chopped
6 plum tomatoes, cut into
    wedges
300ml (½ pint) coconut water
    (swapsies: vegetable stock)

SAUCE
1 tablespoon tomato purée
½ tablespoon fish sauce
    (swapsies: light soy sauce)
¼ teaspoon sea salt flakes
2 teaspoons palm sugar
    (swapsies: soft brown sugar)

It can be a challenge to find a good vegan alternative to fish sauce, a staple in Vietnamese and Thai cuisines. Although there are vegan 'fish' sauce alternatives, they can sometimes be hard to find. Though the flavour will be slightly different, light soy sauce works well in place of fish sauce if you do get stuck.

1. Mix the sauce ingredients together in a small bowl. Heat 3–4 tablespoons of vegetable oil in a large frying pan over a medium-high heat. Add the tofu and cook, turning from time to time, until golden brown on each side, then transfer to a plate lined with kitchen paper to drain off any excess oil.

2. **Build Your Wok Clock:** Start at 12 o'clock with the garlic and roughly chopped spring onions, followed by the tomatoes, the sauce, the fried tofu and lastly the coconut water.

3. Heat 1 tablespoon of vegetable oil in your wok to a medium heat, add the garlic and spring onion and stir-fry for 2–3 minutes until fragrant. Increase the heat to high, then add the tomatoes and cook for 2–3 minutes or so until the skin starts to peel away from the flesh.

4. Add the sauce and bring to a vigorous boil for 1–2 minutes before adding the fried tofu.

5. Reduce the heat to medium and continue to boil for 4–5 minutes. Pour in the coconut water and increase to a high heat to return to the boil for 2–3 minutes. Then reduce the heat again to medium and simmer for 15–20 minutes. Serve garnished with the finely sliced spring onion greens.

SWEET POTATO & PRAWN FRITTERS

PREP: 10 MINS | COOK: 18 MINS | MAKES 10–12 FRITTERS

1 sweet potato, cut into
    3–4cm (1¼–1½ inch) batons
10–12 shell-on raw tiger prawns
vegetable oil
fried mint leaves, to garnish

BATTER
150g (5½oz) rice flour
2 tablespoons cornflour
1 teaspoon ground turmeric
1 teaspoon sea salt flakes
¼ teaspoon ground
    black pepper
240ml (8½fl oz) cold
    sparkling or still water

DIPPING SAUCE
2 garlic cloves,
    finely chopped
juice of ½ lime
1 tablespoon palm sugar
    (swapsies: soft brown
    sugar or honey)
2 tablespoons fish sauce
    or light soy sauce
5 tablespoons water

Much like Ruby – our bubbly Australian wonder of a chef, who is also a presenter on our School of Wok YouTube channel – fritters are fun! They are also a great 'throw it all together and add a batter' sort of food. Whether these *banh tom ho tay* are shallow- or deep-fried, the natural sweet and savoury flavour of the prawns coupled with sweet potato is a match made in heaven. This is a great snack, or starter for a bigger meal.

1. Place all the dry batter ingredients in a mixing bowl, mix together, then very gradually pour in the cold water, stirring until you reach the consistency of single cream. Mix all the dipping sauce ingredients together in a small bowl and stir until the sugar has dissolved.

2. Stir the sweet potato into the batter just before cooking and make sure each piece is well coated. Half-fill a ladle or slotted spoon with the sweet potato batter and place one prawn (with head and shell) on top just before placing the fritter into the pan or wok. Repeat the process ladle by ladle, allowing enough space for each fritter to fry evenly. Deep-fry the fritters in vegetable oil in batches for 5–6 minutes until crisp and golden brown (see page 21), then transfer to a plate lined with kitchen paper to drain off any excess oil. Repeat until all the fritter mixture has been used up.

3. If you prefer to shallow-fry the fritters, heat 5 tablespoons of vegetable oil in a wok or frying pan to a high heat and place each spoonful of mixture into the hot pan with a prawn on top. Reduce the heat to medium and fry for 3–4 minutes or until golden brown around the edges. Flip and cook the other side for a further 2–3 minutes. Repeat until you have used all the mixture.

4. Garnish the fritters with fried mint leaves and serve with the dipping sauce on the side.

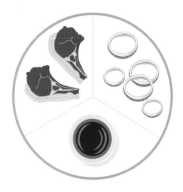

CHARRED & SAUCY PORK CHOPS

PREP: 10 MINS | COOK: 13 MINS | SERVES 4

4 pork chops
½ red onion, finely sliced
vegetable oil
steamed rice, to serve

MARINADE
4 garlic cloves, finely chopped
1 lemon grass stalk, trimmed
   and finely chopped
½ teaspoon Chinese five spice
1 teaspoon sugar
½ teaspoon salt
½ tablespoon oyster sauce
1 tablespoon fish sauce
½ tablespoon light soy sauce

GLAZE
2 tablespoons light soy sauce
1 tablespoon oyster sauce
2 tablespoons tamarind
   concentrate (swapsies:
   juice of ½ lime)
1 tablespoon honey
3-4 tablespoons water

TO GARNISH
1 lime, cut into wedges
finely sliced red onion
handful of coriander leaves

Although it was the first time that I've ever seen Lee, our rock-solid videographer, decline another piece of meat in favour of a break in an air-conditioned iced coffee shop, I'm sure his memory of our time walking through Vietnamese markets (and especially the distinct smell of barbecue pork charring on buckets full of hot coal) will make his tummy rumble. The dish can be found at specialist broken rice stalls, surrounded by queues of hungry office workers at lunchtime. Pounding the pork chops at the beginning ensures they are tender and juicy, so make sure you don't skip this step.

1. Using the back of your cleaver or knife, or a meat mallet, bash the pork chops to tenderize the meat, flattening out each chop for maximum marinade absorption. Pop the chops into a mixing bowl with the marinade ingredients and massage well. Mix the glaze ingredients together in a separate bowl.

2. Preheat the grill to its highest setting. Place the pork chops on a grill rack or roasting tray and cook for 4-5 minutes on each side, turning once and charring well. Once well-charred on both sides and roughly 80 per cent cooked, remove the chops from the grill and allow to rest for 5 minutes.

3. **Build Your Wok Clock:** Start at 12 o'clock with the red onion, followed by the glaze and the partially cooked pork chops.

4. Heat 1 tablespoon of vegetable oil in your wok to a high heat, add the sliced red onion and stir-fry for 30-60 seconds. Bring up to smoking point, then pour in the glaze and bring to a vigorous boil. Once bubbling rapidly, place the chops into the sauce and baste the sauce all over the meat until the chops are fully coated and no sauce remains on the bottom of the wok. Serve with steamed rice, garnished with lime wedges, sliced red onion and coriander leaves.

SPICY CARAMEL-BRAISED FISH

PREP: 10 MINS | COOK: 22 MINS | SERVES 4

4 salmon steaks or catfish steaks
½ red onion, finely chopped
2 garlic cloves, finely chopped
2 spring onions, finely sliced,
    plus extra to serve
1 large red chilli, finely chopped
2 birds' eye chillies, pierced
    with the tip of your knife
vegetable oil

MARINADE
½ red onion, finely chopped
1 garlic clove, finely chopped
1 tablespoon fish sauce
1 tablespoon palm sugar
    (swapsies: soft brown sugar)
½ teaspoon cracked
    black pepper
1 tablespoon sambal
    or Red Curry Paste
    (see pages 188 and 66)
1 tablespoon vegetable oil

CARAMEL
5-6 tablespoons water
2 tablespoons palm sugar
    (swapsies: soft brown sugar)

Ca lok kho to showcases the perfect balance of sweet, savoury and spicy that is one of the characteristics of good Vietnamese cooking. Braising in a spicy caramel sauce helps coat each piece of fish to ensure every bite holds that balance of flavours.

1. Place the fish steaks in a mixing bowl and massage the marinade ingredients into the fish. Mix the caramel ingredients together in a separate bowl.

2. **Build Your Wok Clock:** Start at 12 o'clock with the caramel, followed by the diced red onion and garlic, the spring onions and chillies and the bowl of marinated fish steaks.

3. Heat your wok over a medium heat, pour the caramel mixture into the wok and bring to a boil, allowing the sugar to dissolve and start to caramelize. Once it has turned brown and syrupy in texture, add 1-2 tablespoons of vegetable oil, followed by the diced red onion and garlic. Stir-fry for 30 seconds, then add the spring onions and chillies and continue to fry for another minute.

4. Now gently place the marinated fish steaks into the caramel (reserving any marinade left in the bowl for later) and fry for 2-3 minutes per side, while basting continuously with the sauce. Once both sides are cooked, pour any remaining marinade over the top of the fish and cover the wok with a lid. Keep the wok on a medium heat and boil for 10 minutes. Remove the lid and allow the sauce to simmer and reduce for 2-3 minutes, then serve garnished with spring onion.

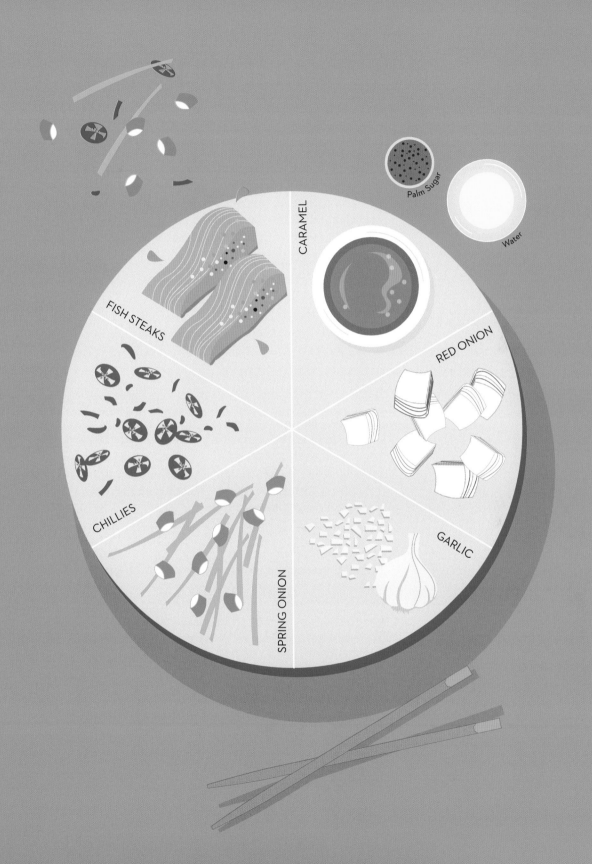

CARAMEL

Palm Sugar

Water

FISH STEAKS

RED ONION

CHILLIES

GARLIC

SPRING ONION

VIETNAMESE EGG MEATLOAF

PREP: 20 MINS, PLUS SOAKING & DRYING | COOK: 50 MINS | SERVES 2-4

small handful of shredded
    dried wood ear mushrooms
    or other dried mushrooms
100g (3½oz) rice vermicelli
1 red onion, finely sliced
vegetable oil
150g (5½oz) minced pork
5 ducks' eggs or 8 hens' eggs
¼ teaspoon salt
¼ teaspoon ground
    black pepper
crunchy vegetables and
    mint sprigs, to serve

MARINADE
¼ teaspoon sugar
1 tablespoon fish sauce

This dish is also a classic offering of broken rice food stalls, along with the Charred & Saucy Pork Chops (see page 104). Imagine a plate of rice piled high with chops, vibrant veggies and stacked slices of eggy meatloaf. A lunch as fit for a king or queen as it is for throngs of office workers, in my eyes.

1. Boil the dried mushrooms in a wok or saucepan of water for 15–20 minutes until tender, then drain through a sieve, squeeze out any excess water and set aside. Soak the vermicelli in hot water for 2–3 minutes until tender, then drain and refresh in cold water. Drain again and spread out on a clean tea towel to dry for 10 minutes, then chop into bite-sized pieces.

2. Lightly fry the onion in 1 tablespoon of oil over a medium heat for 1 minute, then set aside to cool. Place the minced meat in a small bowl and massage in the marinade ingredients.

3. Separate 2 ducks' eggs or 3 hens' eggs. Place the yolks in a small bowl with 1 teaspoon of vegetable oil, and the whites in a mixing bowl. Break the remaining whole eggs into the bowl with the whites, beat well and season with the salt and pepper. Remove as many bubbles from the beaten egg as possible using the edges of a clean sheet of kitchen paper to mop up and absorb.

4. Add the chopped vermicelli, sliced mushrooms and fried red onion to the mixing bowl with the whole eggs and stir well, then add in the marinated meat, breaking it up with your hands and mixing it through. Line a heatproof bowl or a loaf tin with baking paper and pour in the meat mixture. The mixture should be 6–7cm (2½–2¾ inches) deep and the bowl or tin should fit into your steamer.

5. Steam the bowl or tin of meatloaf for 25 minutes (see page 20). Carefully lift the lid off the steamer and pour the beaten egg yolks over the top of the eggy meatloaf, completely covering the surface. Continue to steam for a further 5 minutes, then slice and serve with crunchy vegetables and mint sprigs.

BRAISED COCONUT PORK RIBS

PREP: 15 MINS | COOK: 40 MINS | SERVES 2

300g (10½oz) pork ribs
1 red onion, finely sliced
5 garlic cloves, finely sliced
300ml (½ pint) coconut water
vegetable oil
handful of coriander leaves,
    to garnish

MARINADE
2 tablespoons fish sauce
½ tablespoon oyster sauce
1 tablespoon sugar
½ teaspoon sea salt flakes
½ teaspoon cracked
    black pepper

Here's a one-wok wonder that exudes the simplicity of home cooking and can be made any day of the week. Cutting the pork ribs into small pieces is nice for aesthetics, but also adds ease and pleasure to the eating experience, picking up one bite at a time. Either ask your butcher to chop the pork ribs in half for you, or follow the directions below. Serve with chopsticks, a bowl of rice and a salad or stir-fried veg on the side.

1. If you haven't been able to get the ribs cut up for you, use a cleaver to slice into the meat halfway through each rib, then firmly place your palm over the top of the cleaver and carefully hammer the blade into the bone to cut through it. Alternatively, you could leave the ribs whole if you prefer.

2. Place the ribs into your wok, cover them in boiled water, bring to the boil over a high heat and blanch for 3-4 minutes. Drain the ribs through a sieve and give them a rinse under cold running water, then place in a mixing bowl and massage the marinade ingredients into the meat.

3. **Build Your Wok Clock:** Start at 12 o'clock with the red onion, followed by the garlic, marinated ribs and finally the coconut water.

4. Heat 1 tablespoon of vegetable oil in your wok over a medium heat. Add the red onion and stir-fry for 1-2 minutes, then add the garlic and continue stir-frying for a further minute. Now add the marinated pork ribs and sear for 3-4 minutes until browned slightly around the edges. Increase the heat to high then pour in the coconut water. Bring to a vigorous boil before reducing the heat to low. Simmer, uncovered, for 25-30 minutes or until the sauce is reduced and fully coats and sticks to the ribs. Garnish with coriander leaves and serve.

COCONUT WATER

RED ONION

GARLIC

RIBS

CARAMEL CHICKEN

PREP: 10 MINS | COOK: 35 MINS | SERVES 2

4 chicken thighs,
    with skin and bone
1 thumb-sized piece of ginger,
    peeled and roughly chopped
3 garlic cloves, roughly chopped
2 banana shallots, sliced
    lengthways into wedges
vegetable oil
handful of mint leaves,
    to garnish

BRAISING LIQUID
3 tablespoons palm sugar
    (swapsies: soft brown sugar)
1 teaspoon salt
½ teaspoon black pepper
2½ tablespoons fish sauce
    or light soy sauce

This dish is sticky, sweet, deeply savoury and easy to cook. Make sure you vigorously boil the caramel before adding the water as this will really bring out that wonderful sticky texture when finishing the dish.

1. Halve the chicken thighs by cutting through the bone with a chef's knife or cleaver, leaving the skin intact. Mix the braising liquid ingredients together in a small bowl. Fill a jug with hot water, ready for cooking.

2. **Build Your Wok Clock:** Start at 12 o'clock with the ginger, followed by the garlic, chicken, shallots, braising liquid, and lastly the hot water.

3. Heat 2 tablespoons of vegetable oil in your wok over a medium heat. Add the ginger and stir-fry for 30–60 seconds before adding the garlic. Continue to stir-fry until both the ginger and garlic are golden brown. Add the chicken pieces and sear them skin-side down for 3–4 minutes to crisp up the skin. Then begin to fold the chicken through the aromatics and sear until golden on all sides (5–6 minutes).

4. Add the shallots and fold through for 2–3 minutes before pouring the braising liquid into the wok. Allow the sauce to boil vigorously for 4–5 minutes while folding the chicken through the sauce to coat completely.

5. Then pour the hot water into the wok to roughly two-thirds the depth of the chicken and give it a stir before covering with a lid. Allow to boil over a medium heat for 10 minutes, then remove the lid and boil uncovered for a further 5–8 minutes. The sauce should reduce to a thick, caramel-like consistency, sticky enough to fully coat and cling to the chicken. Serve garnished with mint leaves.

SINGAPOREAN & MALAYSIAN

It may pain those who come from Singapore or Malaysia to see both cuisines put into one chapter. My own experience growing up in Singapore showed me that both Singaporeans and Malaysians, whose culture has had a strong influence on Singaporean cuisine, are extremely passionate about their food. Whether it's laksa, *mee goreng* or *char kway teow* – or simply knowing which tiny food stall in each village makes the best version of each dish – these nations have such passion for their wonderful foods and I commend and admire them both.

I do often ask myself why both cuisines are so moreish and delicious and I think it's because no matter where the influence is from, there is an engrained understanding of how to build a base of savoury flavours into all of their dishes. Both food cultures are heavily influenced by a number of other cuisines and communities including Indian, Malay, Peranakan and Chinese. Out of this assortment of influences, an array of cooking techniques has been created, from South Indian-style curries, to quirky regional takes on traditional Chinese wok dishes, to unique ways of cooking that come directly from the Singaporean and Malaysian communities themselves, such as the famous sesame oil chicken and nasi lemak.

It's the specialist nature of each individual hawker stand or street stall that creates a deep-rooted perfection to the food in both countries. Holidays for me never beat a trip to either country just for the pure fact that you can be strolling down any street and never be more than an arm's length from your next mouth-watering meal or snack! The chefs at these stalls have a true sense of pride in what they do, are quite often extremely relaxed in the kitchen, yet dedicate their lives to cooking the food they love, which creates a unique atmosphere to the 'eating out experience' that is very hard to beat. To me, there is nothing better than sitting on a backless bright-coloured plastic stool next to a stranger slurping their bowl of noodles, watching the stall owners dance around in their goggles, oversized chef jackets, shorts and slippers. I order whatever looks tasty from a close observation of what my fellow surrounding eaters are digging into, usually with their heads deep in their own bowls of deliciousness.

The use of simple local ingredients, such as deep-fried garlic and shallots, calamansi limes, pandan leaves, shrimp paste and prawn stocks, provides depth of flavour to make the originally adopted and adapted curries or stir-fries uniquely Malaysian or Singaporean, carrying that signature savoury flavour throughout the meal. It's these pantry ingredients that I would suggest you explore, as they will help bring that deep flavour profile, ubiquitous in Malaysian and Singaporean cuisines, to your own cooking. However, on many occasions in this chapter, I have suggested alternatives to the more obscure, harder-to-find or stronger ingredients (such as swapping out shrimp paste or *belacan* with a couple of tablespoons of deep-fried shallots or garlic), so that these recipes are accessible to all.

HOKKIEN PRAWN MEE

PREP: 15 MINS, PLUS SOAKING & DRYING | COOK: 35 MINS | SERVES 2

S
I
N
G
A
P
O
R
E
A
N
&
M
A
L
A
Y
S
I
A
N

100g (3½oz) egg noodles
100g (3½oz) rice vermicelli
vegetable oil
10 shell-on raw tiger prawns,
     peeled and deveined
     (heads and shells reserved)
1 egg
handful of Chinese chives
     or Western chives, cut into
     3–4cm (1¼–1½ inch) lengths
handful of beansprouts, rinsed
5–6 garlic cloves, finely chopped
½ tablespoon fish sauce

PRAWN STOCK
heads and shells from
     the prawns (see above)
1 onion, roughly chopped
2 spring onions,
     roughly chopped
1 thumb-sized piece of
     ginger, finely sliced
3–4 garlic cloves, skin on
1 litre (1¾ pints) cold water
     or chicken stock

Watching professional chefs wield a wok is mesmerising.
I recall watching a hawker uncle who cooked his noodles far
longer than I would, hammering more and more stock in as
he went. Unconventional as this may be, the result is heavenly.

1. Soak the egg noodles in hot water for 3–4 minutes until
tender, then drain and refresh in cold water. Drain again and
spread out on a clean tea towel for 10 minutes. Repeat with
the rice vermicelli in a separate bowl, soaking for 2–3 minutes.

2. For the prawn stock, heat 1 tablespoon of oil in a large
saucepan over a medium-high heat and fry all the ingredients,
except the liquid, for 2–3 minutes. Pour the water or stock
over, bring to the boil and allow to simmer for 20 minutes,
skimming the stock every few minutes. Drain through a sieve
over a mixing bowl, discarding the flavouring ingredients,
rinse the pan then return the stock to it and place over a
high heat. Blanch the prawns in the hot stock for 1–2 minutes,
remove with a slotted spoon and transfer to a plate.

3. **Build Your Wok Clock:** Start at 12 o'clock with the egg,
followed by the chives, beansprouts, egg noodles, rice
vermicelli, garlic, fish sauce, prawn stock and prawns.

4. Heat 1 tablespoon of oil in your wok to a medium-high heat,
add the egg and scramble. Add the chives and beansprouts
and stir-fry for 30 seconds. Push the vegetables and egg to
the back of the wok, add another ½ tablespoon of oil and
bring to smoking point, add the egg noodles and stir-fry for
1 minute. Now add the rice vermicelli and stir-fry for 1 minute.

5. Push everything to the back of the wok, add a dash of oil
into the centre followed by the garlic and the fish sauce. Mix
them into the rest of the ingredients then add ½ ladle of stock,
maintaining a high heat. Once the noodles have soaked up
the stock, add another ladle of stock and cook through once
more until absorbed. Lastly, add the prawns to the noodles,
followed by another ladle of stock if required for a glossy
finish. Serve. Freeze the leftover stock for another dish.

SESAME OIL CHICKEN

PREP: 10 MINS | COOK: 30 MINS | SERVES 2

8 chicken wings
2 thumb-sized pieces of
    ginger, peeled and cut
    into matchsticks
2 spring onions,
    roughly chopped
2 star anise
2 tablespoons sesame oil
2 tablespoons ready-made
    crispy fried onions,
    to garnish

MARINADE
1 tablespoon light soy sauce
1 tablespoon Shaoxing rice wine
    (swapsies: dry sherry)
½ teaspoon sugar
½ teaspoon white pepper
1 teaspoon sesame oil
1 tablespoon cornflour

SAUCE
1 tablespoon light soy sauce
1 tablespoon oyster sauce
½ tablespoon dark soy sauce
100ml (3½fl oz) chicken stock

Frying in sesame oil is an unusual choice, mostly because of its low smoking point. However, the popularity of this dish in Singapore shows that sometimes culinary traditions go against scientific law. A thick-based wok or clay pot is crucial here to help control the heat and create a light smokiness or toasted flavour to the chicken when searing in this delicate, yet flavoursome oil.

1. Slice through the joints of the chicken wings to separate the flats and drums, making them easier to fry without using excessive amounts of oil. Place the pieces in a large mixing bowl and massage the marinade ingredients well into the meat, taking care to add the cornflour at the end. Mix the sauce ingredients together in a small bowl.

2. **Build Your Wok Clock:** Start at 12 o'clock with the ginger, most of the spring onion (save some to garnish), star anise, marinated chicken and lastly the sauce.

3. Heat the sesame oil to a medium heat in a heavy-based wok or clay pot. Once hot, add the ginger and spring onion and sizzle for 30–60 seconds before adding the star anise. Next add the chicken and sear in the sesame oil for 6–7 minutes, stirring occasionally yet allowing the chicken to 'catch' and char a bit as it absorbs the smoky sesame oil flavour. Pour the sauce into the wok and bring to a vigorous boil, then cover with a lid and reduce the heat to low. Let it simmer for 15 minutes, lifting the lid to stir every 5 minutes.

4. Once the chicken has cooked through, remove the lid, increase the heat to medium and stir as it cooks for a further 5 minutes until the chicken is fully coated. Serve garnished with crispy fried onions and the reserved spring onion.

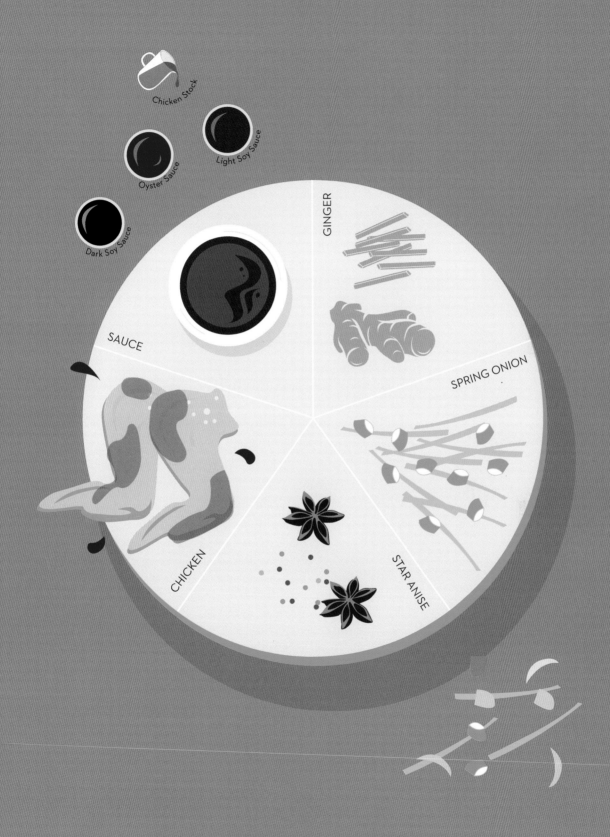

Chicken Stock

Oyster Sauce

Light Soy Sauce

Dark Soy Sauce

SAUCE

GINGER

SPRING ONION

STAR ANISE

CHICKEN

FRIED SARDINES & WATER SPINACH

PREP: 15 MINS | COOK: 15 MINS | SERVES 2

8 whole fresh sardines,
    cleaned and gutted
2 garlic cloves,
    roughly chopped
1 large red chilli,
    roughly chopped
6 tablespoons sambal,
    ready-made or homemade
    (see page 188)
1 bunch of water spinach, cut
    into 4-5cm (1½-2cm) lengths
¼ teaspoon salt
6 hard-boiled eggs, peeled
vegetable oil

SEASONING
2 teaspoons ground turmeric
½ teaspoon sea salt flakes
½ teaspoon white pepper

This dish is often served with boiled eggs cooked in sambal sauce, as it is here, but it would also work a treat with Son in Law Eggs (see page 86). The contrast in textures of the crispy fish and flash-fried water spinach make it a satisfying but simple meal when served with a bowl of steamed rice on the side. Water spinach is also known as *kang kung* or morning glory; you could use pea shoots or spinach instead.

1. Pat the sardines dry by dabbing all over with kitchen paper, then sprinkle with the seasoning ingredients.

2. **Build Your Wok Clock:** Start at 12 o'clock with the sardines, followed by the garlic, chilli, 1 tablespoon of the sambal, the water spinach then the salt. Reserve the remaining sambal and eggs to finish the dish.

3. Deep-fry the coated sardines in vegetable oil at 180°C (350°F) for 5–6 minutes until crispy and golden brown (see page 21). Transfer the fish to a plate lined with kitchen paper. Alternatively, you could shallow-fry the fish if you prefer.

4. If using your wok for deep-frying, carefully pour out the oil into a heatproof bowl to cool and give your wok a quick wipe with kitchen paper. Place the wok back on the hob and bring 1 tablespoon of the fish-cooking oil to a high heat. Add the garlic, chilli and 1 tablespoon of sambal, allowing each ingredient to cook for 30 seconds before adding the next. Add the water spinach and salt and flash-fry for 1–2 minutes then transfer the vegetables to a plate.

5. Return the wok to the hob over a medium heat. Add the remaining sambal and bring to the boil before adding the peeled eggs. Fold them through the sambal to coat and warm through for 2–3 minutes, then serve alongside the fish and vegetables.

SATAY SAUCE

PREP: 10 MINS | COOK: 23 MINS | MAKES 400–500ML (14–18FL OZ)

150g (5½oz) salted
    roasted peanuts
vegetable oil

SPICES
6 large red chillies,
    finely chopped
1 red onion, finely chopped
1 lemon grass stalk, trimmed,
    bruised and finely chopped
1 thumb-sized piece of
    galangal or ginger, peeled
    and finely chopped
3 garlic cloves, finely chopped

SAUCE
1 teaspoon salt
1 teaspoon palm sugar
    (swapsies: soft brown sugar)
2 tablespoons lime juice or
    tamarind concentrate
5 tablespoons kecap manis
    (sweet soy sauce)
200ml (7fl oz) coconut water
200ml (7fl oz) hot water

There are roads named after satay in Singapore, and whole streets lined with satay stalls all over Malaysia – and it's the peanut sauce that makes this famous dish so moreish. My advice is to make a whole batch of this sauce, then freeze any you don't use for later. Defrost the frozen sauce when you need it by placing in a small pan with a little hot water and bring to the boil. Serve the sauce in the classic way with marinated meat (see page 126), or more simply with fried fish and steamed rice for a quick and tasty dinner.

1. Blitz the roasted peanuts into a fine powder in a food processor or crush using a pestle and mortar. Mix the spices together in a bowl or blitz them all together in a food processor if you prefer. Mix the sauce ingredients together in another bowl.

2. **Build Your Wok Clock:** Start at 12 o'clock with the spices, followed by the peanuts and lastly the sauce.

3. Heat 4–5 tablespoons of vegetable oil in your wok over a medium-low heat and add the spices into the oil once hot. Gently stir-fry for 4–5 minutes until fragrant. Add the crushed peanuts, stir in well and fry for 2–3 minutes. Next pour the sauce in and bring to the boil. Reduce the heat and simmer for 10–15 minutes or until thickened to the desired consistency.

4. In parts of Malaysia the satay sauce is thin and 'soupy' – I love this texture as it's just about thick enough to coat the meat or veg, but also thin enough to drink up every last drop. In other parts of the world, satay sauce is thicker and used mainly for dipping. Either way, it's the base spices and a perfect mix of sweet, spicy and salty that makes this sauce so tasty, so aim for whatever consistency you prefer.

Kecap Manis

Palm Sugar

Hot Water

Coconut Water

Salt

Lime Juice

SPICES

SAUCE

PEANUTS

WOK-FRIED SATAY

PREP: 10 MINS | COOK: 18 MINS | SERVES 2

450g (1lb) boneless pork
    shoulder, skinless, boneless
    chicken thighs or rump steak
    (or a mixture)
vegetable oil

MARINADE
3 garlic cloves, finely chopped
1 lemon grass stalk, trimmed,
    bruised and finely chopped
½ onion, finely chopped
2 teaspoons Madras
    curry powder
½ teaspoon chilli powder
½ tablespoon honey
1½ tablespoons light soy sauce
1 tablespoon vegetable oil

TO SERVE
1 cucumber, cut into
    bite-sized chunks
1 lime, cut into wedges
Satay Sauce (see page 124)

Classic satay as we know it is usually served on a stick, which makes it fun as a street food, but not necessarily practical for an everyday mid-week meal. If you love satay as much as I do, there's no reason to deprive yourself for the sake of the time taken to skewer each piece of meat. Just get your wok as hot as possible, sear away, and then let your guests do the dipping and skewering themselves.

1. Slice the meat into 3mm- (⅛ inch-) thick bite-sized pieces and bash well with the side of your cleaver or a rolling pin to flatten it out. Blitz the marinade ingredients in a food processor or pound using a pestle and mortar until smooth, pouring in the soy sauce and vegetable oil last. Pour the marinade over the meat and massage well. Set aside for 10–15 minutes to marinate, or cover and chill in the fridge overnight if preparing in advance.

2. Place the sliced cucumber in a bowl of cold water in the fridge until ready to serve.

3. Treating the wok more like a hot plate, rub 1–2 tablespoons of oil all around the inside and place over a high heat. Once smoking hot, lay some of the flattened pieces of meat in the wok with a little space between them as if laying pieces of bacon in a frying pan. Press into the meat with a spatula to sear well on one side for 2–3 minutes. Once charred, turn the pieces of meat with a pair of tongs and sear the other side for a further 2–3 minutes.

4. Repeat this process until all the meat has been charred, transferring the cooked meat to a roasting tray in a low oven to keep warm while the remaining batches are cooking. Serve the meat piled high on a platter with a heap of cucumber, the lime wedges and satay sauce on the side. You could add a few skewers or toothpicks scattered around for easy picking and fun family eating.

CHAR KWAY TEOW

PREP: 15 MINS, PLUS SOAKING AND DRYING
COOK: 10 MINS | SERVES 2

150g (5½oz) flat rice noodles
2 eggs, lightly beaten
1 spring onion, roughly chopped
3-4 garlic cloves, finely sliced
handful of Chinese chives or
    wild garlic, cut into 3-4cm
    (1¼-1½ inch) lengths
handful of beansprouts, rinsed
12 raw peeled tiger prawns,
    deveined and sliced in half
vegetable oil
handful of coriander leaves and
    finely sliced chilli, to garnish

SAUCE

1-2 teaspoons sambal,
    ready-made or homemade
    (see page 188), or chilli paste
½ tablespoon oyster sauce
1 tablespoon light soy sauce
3 tablespoons kecap manis
    (sweet soy sauce)
½ ladle of chicken stock
½ teaspoon salt

The fact that it only costs around 5 Malaysian ringgit
(about 85p/$1.25) for a plate of these noodles is one of the
reasons I return to Malaysia for holidays time and time again.
You could close your eyes and dream you are on the seafront
at a street-side joint in Penang, just make sure in your dream
that you've got the right currency in your pocket or you'll
have to cook it yourself.

1. Soak the noodles in hot water for 6-8 minutes until tender,
then drain and refresh in cold water. Drain again and spread
out on a clean tea towel to dry for 10 minutes. Mix the sauce
ingredients together in a bowl.

2. **Build Your Wok Clock:** Start at 12 o'clock with the beaten
eggs, followed by the spring onion, garlic, Chinese chives,
beansprouts, prawns, noodles and lastly the sauce.

3. Heat 2 tablespoons of vegetable oil in your wok over a
high heat. Once smoking hot, add the beaten egg and allow
to bubble up before pushing into it gently to scramble. Once
the egg is half cooked, fold over and push to the back of the
wok. Add ½ tablespoon of vegetable oil to the wok and then
add the spring onion, garlic, Chinese chives, beansprouts
and prawns one at a time, stir-frying for 30 seconds between
each addition.

4. Push all the ingredients to the back of the wok once more,
add ½-1 tablespoon of vegetable oil and bring to a smoking
point. Add the noodles, then fold the vegetables into the
centre of the noodles and continue stir-frying for 30-60
seconds. Keeping a high heat, pour the sauce into the wok.
Give your wok a vigorous shake, while stirring with your ladle
or spatula to distribute the sauce evenly throughout the
noodles. Continue to stir-fry for 2-3 minutes until the sauce
evenly coats all the ingredients, and the noodles start to soften.
As soon as the sauce has been fully absorbed by the noodles
and they start to catch slightly on the bottom of the wok,
garnish with coriander and sliced red chilli and serve.

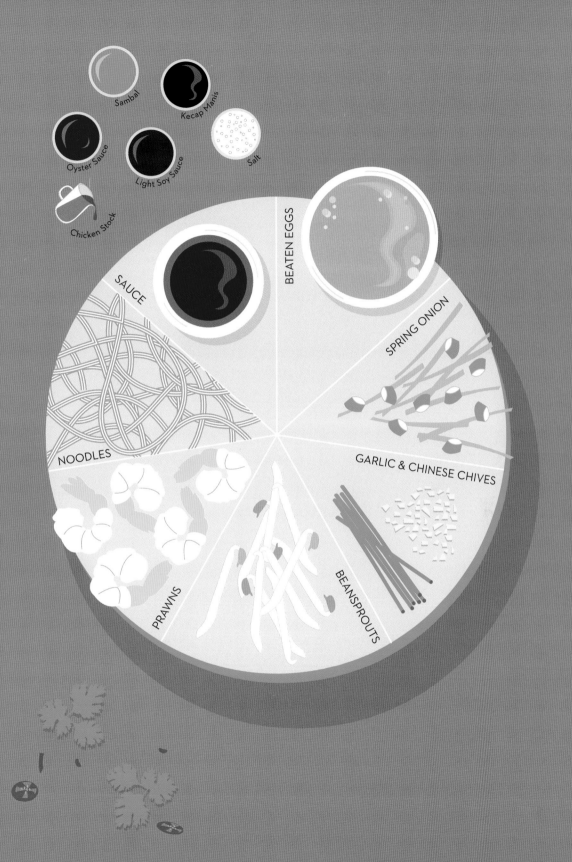

Sambal

Kecap Manis

Oyster Sauce

Light Soy Sauce

Salt

Chicken Stock

SAUCE

BEATEN EGGS

SPRING ONION

NOODLES

GARLIC & CHINESE CHIVES

PRAWNS

BEANSPROUTS

NASI LEMAK

PREP: 30 MINS | COOK: 45 MINS | SERVES 2

6 chicken thighs, with skin
and bone
1 tablespoon unsalted butter
1 large red onion, finely chopped
½ thumb-sized piece of ginger,
peeled and roughly chopped
3 garlic cloves, roughly chopped
½ x 400ml (14oz) can of
chopped tomatoes
1 tablespoon vegetable oil
handful of coriander leaves,
to garnish

WHOLE SPICES
3 birds' eye chillies, pierced
with the tip of your knife
1 lemon grass stalk, trimmed
and bruised
4 lime leaves (optional)
1 cinnamon stick
3–4 cloves
2 teaspoons cumin seeds

GROUND SPICES
1 teaspoon ground turmeric
½ teaspoon chilli powder
1 teaspoon salt

STOCK
2 teaspoons tomato purée
150ml (¼ pint) coconut milk
100ml (3½fl oz) chicken stock

TO SERVE
Coconut Rice (see page 187)
½ cucumber, sliced
2 tablespoons sambal,
ready-made or homemade
(see page 188), or chilli paste
2 soft-boiled eggs, halved
handful of roasted peanuts

There are several parts to this mixed-rice dish, so I would recommend leaving it for the weekend when you're less pressed for time. Boil a couple of extra eggs at breakfast, save some cucumber from your lunchtime salad, and make your coconut rice early on so that you can just focus on the chicken curry for this epic family feast. I always recommend having sambal and peanuts within easy snacking reach anyway, and they make great accompaniments to this dish.

1. Halve the chicken thighs by cutting through the bone with a chef's knife or cleaver, leaving the skin intact. Place the whole spices in one bowl and the ground spices in another, then mix the stock ingredients together in a jug.

2. **Build Your Wok Clock:** Start at 12 o'clock with the chicken, followed by the whole spices, red onion, ginger, garlic, ground spices, chopped tomatoes, and lastly the jug of stock.

3. Heat the vegetable oil and butter together in your wok over a high heat. Place the chicken skin-side down in the wok and sear for 3–4 minutes until browned and crispy. Fold through and stir-fry for a further 3–4 minutes until fully cooked, then remove from the wok and set aside.

4. Reduce the heat to medium and add the whole spices to the wok. Stir-fry for 1–2 minutes before adding the red onion, ginger and garlic. Stir-fry for 4–5 minutes until the onion turns brick red, then add the ground spices followed by the chicken. Fold all the ingredients together to coat the chicken with the spices and flavours. Increase the heat to high then pour in the chopped tomatoes and bring to a vigorous boil. Give the curry a stir and allow to boil for 10 minutes.

5. Pour in the jug of stock and return to a vigorous boil. Reduce the heat to medium and simmer for 20 minutes. If you haven't prepared the serving ingredients already, use this time to do so. Serve your coconut rice with a good ladle of the curry, garnished with coriander, and the rest of the accompaniments on the side.

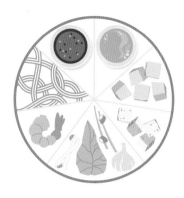

1 potato, peeled and cut
into 2cm (¾ inch) cubes
6–8 raw peeled tiger prawns,
deveined (optional)
2 eggs, well beaten
100g (3½oz) deep-fried
tofu pieces (tofu pok),
halved diagonally
2 garlic cloves, finely sliced
1 spring onion, roughly chopped
2 sweetheart cabbage leaves,
chopped into chunks
large handful of
beansprouts, rinsed
200g (7oz) fresh egg noodles
or wonton noodles
vegetable oil

SAUCE

½ teaspoon curry powder
2 teaspoons sambal,
ready-made or homemade
(see page 188), or chilli paste
½ teaspoon salt
1 teaspoon sugar
1½ tablespoons light soy sauce
1 tablespoon kecap manis
(sweet soy sauce)
½ tablespoon lime juice or
Worcestershire sauce
1 tablespoon tomato ketchup

TO GARNISH

handful of salted roasted peanuts
handful of ready-made crispy
fried onions
finely sliced red chilli
small handful of coriander leaves
lime wedges

MAMAK FRIED NOODLES

PREP: 20 MINS | COOK: 24 MINS | SERVES 2

Malaysian-Indian street stands (*mamak* stalls) are found across Malaysia and will each have their own version of *mee goreng* (fried noodles). It's a dish that's known for its spicy but not overpowering flavours, well balanced by the addition of sweet soy or kecap manis.

1. Boil the potato cubes in a pan of boiling water for 6–8 minutes until softened, yet still holding their shape. Drain and allow to cool. If using prawns, blanch them in boiling water for 2 minutes then drain. Mix the sauce ingredients together in a small bowl.

2. **Build Your Wok Clock:** Start at 12 o'clock with the eggs, followed by the cooked potato, tofu, garlic, spring onion, cabbage, beansprouts, prawns, noodles and lastly the sauce.

3. Heat 2 tablespoons of vegetable oil in your wok over a high heat. Pour in the eggs and allow to bubble up and then fold through and gently scramble. Push the egg to the side of the wok, add another ½ tablespoon of vegetable oil and bring to smoking point. Place the potatoes into the wok, fold the egg over the top of the potatoes and fry for 3–4 minutes, turning occasionally. Once the potatoes are crisp and brown on all sides, add the tofu and continue to stir-fry for 1–2 minutes. Add the garlic, spring onion, cabbage, beansprouts and prawns to the wok, stir-frying for 30 seconds before adding each new ingredient.

4. Stir-fry for a further 2 minutes, then add the noodles and stir-fry for 1 minute more. Bring the wok up to smoking point, then add the sauce and bring to a vigorous boil. Carefully fold the noodles through the sauce, keeping them intact. Continue to stir-fry for 1–2 minutes until the noodles are fully coated and the sauce is evenly distributed and absorbed. Serve scattered generously with the garnishes.

REALLY TASTY FISH CURRY

PREP: 15 MINS | COOK: 30 MINS | SERVES 3-4

20 fresh curry leaves
1 red onion, sliced
5 garlic cloves, roughly chopped
2 large green chillies, pierced
   with the tip of your knife
2 teaspoons curry powder
½ teaspoon chilli powder
2 tomatoes, cut into wedges
1 teaspoon salt
½ teaspoon palm sugar
   (swapsies: soft brown sugar)
3-4 salmon steaks
2 handfuls of okra
vegetable oil

WHOLE SPICES
(*HALBAR CAMPUR*)
2 teaspoons fenugreek seeds
1 teaspoon fennel seeds
1 teaspoon mustard seeds
2 tablespoons urid dal

STOCK
1 tablespoon tamarind
   concentrate
3 tablespoons yogurt
300ml (½ pint) coconut milk
500ml (18fl oz) water
   or chicken stock

Kare ikan (curried fish) is a ubiquitous aromatic delight that touches every part of Malaysia – you just can't miss it! Our very new chef tutor Ryan got thrown in the deep end with this, and he did a great job of cooking a stack of large salmon steaks in a tiny heavy-based wok, with the added pressure of me watching over his wok shoulder. Safe to say, Ryan's salmon made it without any breakages at all and doesn't it look delicious? Not just tasty, but *really* tasty.

1. Mix the whole spices together in a small bowl, then stir the stock ingredients together in a jug.

2. **Build Your Wok Clock:** Start at 12 o'clock with the whole spices, followed by the curry leaves, onion, garlic, chillies, curry powder, chilli powder, tomatoes, salt, sugar, salmon steaks, the stock and lastly the whole okra.

3. Heat 2-3 tablespoons of oil in your wok over a medium heat. Add the whole spices and cover with a lid. After a minute or so, the mustard seeds will start to pop, hitting the base of the lid. Once the popping has stopped, remove the lid and add the curry leaves, onion and garlic, stir-frying for 30 seconds before adding each new ingredient. Then add the chillies, curry powder and chilli powder and stir. Next add the tomatoes, salt and sugar, stir once, cover with a lid and cook for 5 minutes to allow the juices to release from the tomatoes.

4. Remove the lid and press into the tomato wedges with a spoon to bring out more moisture. Then add the salmon and increase the heat to high. Carefully fold the spicy sauce over the fish steaks to coat well before pouring the stock over the fish and bringing to a vigorous boil. Reduce the heat to medium and simmer for 15 minutes. Add the okra to the top of the curry, simmer for a further 5 minutes and serve.

VEGAN LAKSA

PREP: 20 MINS, PLUS SOAKING | COOK: 35 MINS | SERVES 2

4–5 lime leaves
400ml (14fl oz) can
   of coconut milk
100g (3½oz) deep-fried
   tofu pieces (*tofu pok*),
   halved diagonally
200g (7oz) rice vermicelli
handful of sugarsnaps
1 carrot, finely sliced
100g (3½oz) beansprouts,
   rinsed
vegetable oil

CURRY PASTE
8–10 dried red chillies
2 teaspoons cumin seeds
2 teaspoons coriander seeds
1 teaspoon ground turmeric
½ red onion, finely chopped
½ thumb-sized piece of ginger,
   peeled and finely chopped
3 garlic cloves, finely chopped
2 lemon grass stalks, trimmed,
   bruised and finely chopped

STOCK
500ml (18fl oz) coconut water
500ml (18fl oz) vegetable stock
1 tablespoon palm sugar
   (swapsies: soft brown sugar)
4 tablespoons light soy sauce
½ teaspoon sea salt flakes

TO GARNISH
lime wedges
handful of coriander
sliced red chilli
1 tablespoon sambal,
   ready-made or homemade
   (see page 188) (optional)

For me, a laksa is the perfect quick-win vehicle to use up any leftover curry as you can easily use it in place of the homemade curry paste. Though it won't hold a candle to the laksa aunties of Malaysia, it will make an easy, tasty dinner, so feel free to give it a try with this recipe. If you do make the curry paste, use at least 3–4 tablespoons in your laksa (or more if you wish), then freeze the rest for another day.

1. If making the curry paste, soak the dried red chillies in hot water for 10 minutes, drain and finely chop. Pound all the curry paste ingredients using a pestle and mortar until smooth. Stir the stock ingredients together in a jug.

2. **Build Your Wok Clock:** Start at 12 o'clock with the curry paste or leftover curry, followed by the lime leaves, coconut milk, the stock, tofu, rice vermicelli, sugarsnaps, carrot and lastly the beansprouts.

3. Heat 2 tablespoons of oil in your wok to a medium heat. Add 3–4 tablespoons of curry paste (or 5–6 tablespoons of leftover curry) and stir-fry for 4–5 minutes until it deepens in colour. Now add the lime leaves and one-quarter of the coconut milk and bring to a vigorous boil. Stir well, scraping off any paste stuck to the bottom of the wok and then add a further quarter of the coconut milk. Return to a boil before adding the remaining coconut milk to the wok. Pour in the stock and return to a boil once again. Next add the tofu pieces, reduce the heat to medium and simmer for 15–20 minutes until the flavour deepens and the stock reduces.

4. To finish the soup, add the vermicelli and boil for 3–4 minutes before fishing it out with tongs or a slotted spoon and dividing between serving bowls. Add the sugarsnaps and carrot to the soup and boil for 2–3 minutes. Scoop the veg out of the soup and place on top of the noodles. Next, dunk the beansprouts into the hot soup for 30 seconds. Scoop out the tofu into the serving bowls, followed by the just-cooked beansprouts on top. Pour the broth over the bowls of noodles and veg and scatter the garnishes over the top.

INDONESIAN
& PINOY

Moving from one chapter to the next feels like crossing the border into another country as migrating people have done for thousands of years, with similarities and influences being carried with them and adopted where they settle. While it's easy to see the similarities between Singaporean and Malaysian cuisines and their numerous influences, traditional Indonesian and Malay food also share a lot of techniques and base sauces used in both cuisines. The Satay Sauce (see page 124) from the last chapter, for example, is a versatile mixture made with ingredients shared across both cultures and easily lends itself to many different types of cooking. You could cross the border from Bornean Sabah (in East Malaysia) to Indonesian Borneo and be fed a very similar family sambal as a side dish, or as a base to a hearty Indonesian or Malaysian meal.

With its equatorial climate and archipelago existence, Indonesia produces some of the finest fruit and produce in the world. The islands are full of beautiful seafood and fish. I can remember the long boat trips we used to take out to sea when I was younger. With the help of local fishermen, we would put a simple fishing line in and, minutes later, pull out tens of sprats or local mackerel, which we would then use as bait to catch deep-sea grouper, big enough to serve twenty. Aside from all the fish and fruits, sambal stands out as the national food of Indonesia, with so many different variations used as a condiment, but also as a base flavour for many dishes. You can find an extremely tasty and versatile homemade sambal recipe later on in the book (see page 188). Use it in any of the recipes that require sambal and you will see that most of the work of creating a flavourful dish will already be done for you as your sambal will already be so tasty and full of flavour.

Just northeast of Borneo and Indonesia lies the neighbouring archipelago of the Philippines. For some reason, Filipino or Pinoy cuisine has not had quite the same glory or exposure as its neighbours, yet the food is unique and deserves to be talked about more. This chapter gives a nod to a selection of some of the most popular and delicious Pinoy dishes. You will notice the Philippines has had heavy influence from the Spanish, Americans and Japanese during their periods of occupation through the country's history. For example, many salads and fruit salads are covered in salad cream or mayonnaise. The dishes I have focussed on here are heartier, home-style, comforting meals that are very simple to cook in a wok and equally as delicious. I hope that cooking these recipes will inspire you to try more Pinoy food whenever you have the chance.

FRIED TEMPEH WITH SATAY SAUCE

PREP: 10 MINS, PLUS MARINATING | COOK: 9 MINS | SERVES 2

400g (14oz) fresh tempeh
   or firm tofu, cut into
   bite-sized cubes
vegetable oil
½ quantity of Satay Sauce
   (see page 124), to serve
½ cucumber, chopped into
   chunks, to serve
1 red onion, chopped into
   chunks, to serve

MARINADE
2 garlic cloves
1 large red chilli
½ lemon grass stalk, trimmed
½ teaspoon ground turmeric
1 teaspoon curry powder
1 tablespoon light soy sauce
½ tablespoon palm sugar
   (swapsies: soft brown sugar)
1 teaspoon sesame oil
50ml (2fl oz) coconut water

A uniquely Indonesian invention, tempeh is a soybean-based protein which is naturally sweet with a depth of sour and a hint of bitterness. These flavours match perfectly with the flavours of satay. Here's a simple stir-fry to put homemade Satay Sauce (see page 124) to good use. We used handmade tempeh from our brilliant 'Tempeh Man', Will, but it's readily available in larger supermarkets too.

1. Blitz the marinade ingredients together in a food processor or pound using a pestle and mortar until smooth, adding the coconut water at the end. Pour this over the tempeh pieces in a bowl and massage well, taking care not to break up the pieces. Set aside for 10–15 minutes to marinate, or cover and chill in the fridge overnight if preparing in advance.

2. Heat 3–4 tablespoons of vegetable oil in your wok over a medium-high heat. Place the marinated tempeh into the hot oil, reserving any additional marinade in the bowl for later. Stir-fry for 5–6 minutes to crisp up and char the edges of the tempeh, then carefully pour any excess oil out of the wok into a heatproof bowl and increase the heat to high.

3. Once smoking hot, pour the reserved marinade into the wok and bring to a vigorous boil. Gently fold the tempeh through the boiling marinade for 2–3 minutes until all the liquid has fully evaporated and the marinade has coated the tempeh. Serve the tempeh with the satay sauce, cucumber and red onion on the side.

2 eggs, well beaten
1 garlic clove, finely chopped
½ red pepper, finely chopped
handful of asparagus spears,
    trimmed and chopped
250g (9oz) cooked rice,
    at room temperature
vegetable oil
finely chopped spring onion,
    to garnish

SAUCE

1 teaspoon sambal, ready-made
    or homemade (see page 188),
    or chilli paste (optional)
1 teaspoon tomato purée
½ tablespoon light soy sauce
1 tablespoon kecap manis
    (sweet soy sauce)
½ teaspoon sesame oil
salt and pepper

NASI GORENG

PREP: 10 MINS | COOK: 10 MINS | SERVES 2

Rice is a symbol of life in many Asian countries; it's the base carbohydrate that seems to keep us all going. The best thing about it is its versatility – there are so many different grains and various ways of cooking it! When frying rice, you can put whatever you want into the stir-fry and have dinner served in a matter of minutes.

1. Mix the sauce ingredients together in a small bowl and season with salt and pepper.

2. **Build Your Wok Clock:** Start at 12 o'clock with the eggs, followed by the garlic, red pepper, asparagus, cooked rice and lastly the sauce.

3. Heat 2 tablespoons of vegetable oil in your wok over a high heat. Once smoking hot, pour the eggs into the oil and allow to bubble up before breaking them up and scrambling them. Push the egg to the back of the wok and then add the garlic, red pepper and asparagus, stir-frying for 30 seconds between adding each new ingredient.

4. Push all the veg to the back of the wok, add ½ tablespoon of vegetable oil and bring to a smoking point before adding the rice. Break up any clumps of rice by pushing down on them against the wok with a spatula or ladle. Fold the vegetables and egg into the rice to combine and stir-fry for 1–2 minutes. Then pour the sauce over the rice and continue to stir-fry for a further 2 minutes. Some of the rice should begin to crisp up for added texture and flavour. Garnish with spring onion and serve.

BEN'S SPICY FRIED CHICKEN

PREP: 15 MINS, PLUS SOAKING | COOK: 18 MINS | SERVES 2–3

3 whole chicken legs, with
    skin and bone, thighs and
    drumsticks separated
8–10 tablespoons cornflour
vegetable oil

SPICE PASTE
10 dried chillies
1 teaspoon ground cumin
1 teaspoon ground coriander
½ tablespoon curry powder
1 teaspoon ground turmeric
½ tablespoon fennel seeds
½ red onion, finely chopped
4 garlic cloves, finely chopped
1 thumb-sized piece of galangal
    or ginger, peeled and
    finely chopped
2 lemon grass stalks, trimmed,
    bruised and finely chopped
1 teaspoon salt

CHILLI OIL
5 tablespoons vegetable oil
1 red onion, finely chopped
5 garlic cloves, finely chopped
5 large green chillies,
    finely chopped
5 large red chillies,
    finely chopped
handful of coriander stalks,
    finely chopped
1 teaspoon salt

One of our business partners, Ben, has been wanting to have a face-to-face meeting for over a year now just so that he can get his well-deserved fix of spicy fried chicken. Unfortunately, the closest he's managed to get is his local chicken shop. Deep-fried chicken is the epitome of comfort food and the Indonesians have perfected it. Drop the ketchup and replace it with this spicy marinade, topped off with the salty chilli oil just to make you drool that little bit more.

1. To make the spice paste, soak the dried red chillies in hot water for 10 minutes, then drain and finely chop. Pound with all the remaining spice paste ingredients using a pestle and mortar or blend together in a food processor until you have a smooth paste.

2. Place the chicken pieces into a large mixing bowl and massage the paste into the meat to fully coat. Just before cooking, coat the chicken with cornflour, ensuring that each piece is evenly dusted with a thin layer of flour completely covering the skin.

3. Deep-fry the coated chicken in vegetable oil at 180°C (350°F) for 1 minute (see page 21), then reduce the heat to medium-low, so that the oil is just simmering. Continue to cook for 10–15 minutes, depending on the thickness of the pieces.

4. While your chicken is cooking, heat a heavy-based wok or saucepan over a medium heat. Once smoking hot, add all the chilli oil ingredients and stir-fry for 5–6 minutes until the chillies have softened slightly. Tip into a ramekin or small bowl to serve.

5. When the chicken is cooked through, increase the heat to medium-high and fry for a further 2 minutes for a really crispy skin. The chicken is ready when the pieces begin to float freely to the top of the oil. Transfer the chicken to a plate lined with kitchen paper, then serve with the chilli oil to drizzle over or dip.

CHICKEN ADOBO

PREP: 10 MINS, PLUS MARINATING | COOK: 40 MINS | SERVES 2-3

3 whole chicken legs with
 skin and bone, thighs and
 drumsticks separated
1 red onion, finely chopped
2 garlic cloves, roughly chopped
1 teaspoon black peppercorns
3 bay leaves
350ml (12fl oz) chicken stock
 or water
vegetable oil
steamed rice, to serve

MARINADE
2 garlic cloves, roughly chopped
3 tablespoons palm sugar
 (swapsies: soft brown sugar)
100ml (3½fl oz) rice vinegar
125ml (4fl oz) light soy sauce
1 tablespoon dark soy sauce

Adobo is considered to be the national dish of the Philippines. This simple dish is usually cooked with pork belly or chicken, or both mixed together. Braising the meat creates a sticky, moreish glaze, which is also great for slathering over a bowl of steamed rice.

1. Place the chicken pieces into a large mixing bowl and massage the marinade ingredients into the meat to fully coat. Set aside for 10 minutes.

2. **Build Your Wok Clock:** Start at 12 o'clock with the marinated chicken, followed by the red onion, garlic, black peppercorns, bay leaves and lastly the chicken stock or water.

3. Heat 1-2 tablespoons of vegetable oil in your wok over a medium heat. Place the marinated chicken skin-side down into the wok, reserving any marinade left in the bowl. Sear the chicken for 5-6 minutes until the skin is crisp and golden brown. Turn over and sear the other side for 3-4 minutes, then add the red onion and garlic around the sides of the chicken pieces and fry for 2-3 minutes in the excess oil.

4. Add the black peppercorns and bay leaves and increase the heat to high. Once smoking hot, pour the remaining marinade over the chicken and bring to a vigorous boil for 4-5 minutes, basting the chicken with sauce every so often. Next pour the chicken stock or water over the top of the chicken and return to the boil. Reduce the heat to medium-low and allow to simmer for 20-25 minutes, uncovered, until the sauce reduces right down to a sticky, glossy glaze. Serve over rice.

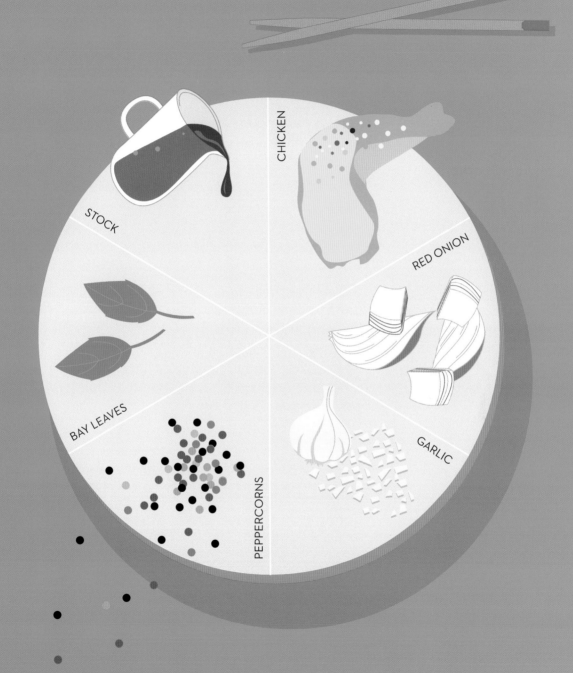

CHICKEN

STOCK

RED ONION

BAY LEAVES

GARLIC

PEPPERCORNS

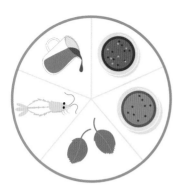

SAMBAL PRAWNS

PREP: 15 MINS | COOK: 21 MINS | SERVES 2

400g (14oz) shell-on raw
 tiger prawns
150ml (5fl oz) Sambal Paste
 (see page 188)
6 lime leaves
100ml (3½fl oz) chicken stock
 or water
vegetable oil

SAMBAL LIQUID
2 tablespoons tamarind
 concentrate or lime juice
1 teaspoon salt
2 teaspoons palm sugar
 (swapsies: soft brown sugar)
1 tablespoon dark soy sauce
5 tablespoons water

Chilli, garlic and prawns are a match made in heaven. The citrusy, sweet and sour notes from the lime leaves and sambal in this dish help to further accentuate the savoury flavours of the prawns. This recipe is usually cooked with shell-on prawns, but can easily be made with peeled and deveined prawns to save time.

1. Mix the sambal liquid ingredients together in a bowl.

2. Peel the bodies of the prawns, but keep the heads on. Use a toothpick to remove the veins by poking it through the flesh behind the vein, then pulling up and away from the flesh to dislodge the vein – you can then pull to remove it fully.

3. **Build Your Wok Clock:** Start at 12 o'clock with the sambal paste, followed by the sambal liquid, the lime leaves, prawns and lastly the chicken stock.

4. Heat 5–6 tablespoons of vegetable oil in your wok over a medium heat. Add the sambal paste, then decrease the heat to low and fry for 6–7 minutes until the paste turns a dark orange-brown.

5. Now add the sambal liquid and stir-fry for 8–10 minutes until jammy, thick and sticky. Add the lime leaves and prawns to the wok and stir-fry for 1–2 minutes. Increase the heat and, once smoking hot, pour the chicken stock or water into the wok. Bring to the boil and simmer for 2 minutes more over a high heat. Once the prawns have turned coral-pink, the dish is ready to serve.

PINOY GARLIC BUTTER CHILLI PRAWNS

PREP: 15 MINS | COOK: 6 MINS | SERVES 2

12–15 shell-on raw tiger prawns
4 tablespoons salted butter
6 garlic cloves, roughly chopped
½ teaspoon chilli powder
1 large red chilli, sliced
1 tomato, cut into wedges
coriander leaves, to garnish

SAUCE
4 tablespoons banana ketchup
    (swapsies: tomato ketchup)
150ml (¼ pint) lemonade
    or ginger beer
½ teaspoon sea salt flakes
½ teaspoon white pepper

Banana ketchup is a popular condiment in the Philippines, first produced during WWII due to a tomato shortage. If you can get hold of it, then it's definitely worth a try! If not, then everyday tomato ketchup works too. The dish is simple, sweet, saucy and oozing in garlic butter, so be prepared to lick the prawn shells and plate clean.

1. Use a toothpick to remove the veins from the prawns by poking it in the gap between the head and body shell, through the flesh behind the vein, then pulling up and away from the flesh to dislodge the vein – you can then pull to remove it fully. Snip any sharp edges off the heads with a pair of scissors. Mix the sauce ingredients together in a bowl.

2. **Build Your Wok Clock:** Start at 12 o'clock with half the butter, half the chopped garlic, the chilli powder, red chilli, prawns, tomato wedges, the sauce, the remaining butter and the rest of the garlic.

3. Heat the first half of the butter in your wok over a medium heat and immediately add the first half of the garlic, followed by the chilli powder and chillies. Stir-fry for 30 seconds then add in the prawns. Sear the prawns and fold through for 1–2 minutes. Increase the heat to high and add the tomatoes. Continue stir-frying for 30–60 seconds, until the tomato skins start to blister and the juices are released.

4. Pour the sauce into the wok and bring to a vigorous boil. Once the prawns are coral-pink in colour, remove from the wok onto a serving plate.

5. Give your wok a quick clean under the hot tap then return to the hob to dry over a medium heat. Once dry, add the remaining butter. Once melted, add the remaining garlic and fry for 30 seconds before pouring over the top of the prawns to finish. Garnish with coriander leaves.

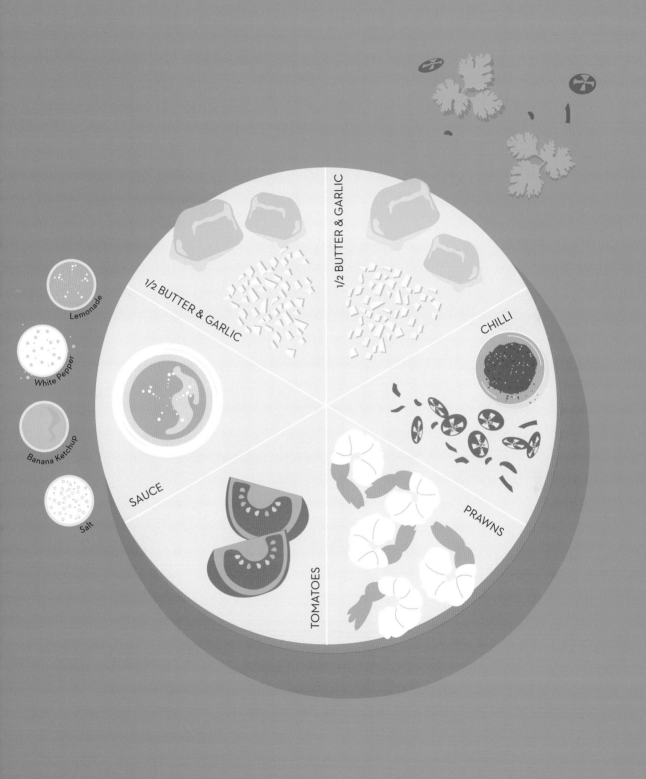

Lemonade

White Pepper

Banana Ketchup

Salt

1/2 BUTTER & GARLIC

1/2 BUTTER & GARLIC

CHILLI

SAUCE

PRAWNS

TOMATOES

COCONUT SPICY SQUASH STEW

PREP: 12 MINS | COOK: 33 MINS | SERVES 2

3–4 garlic cloves, finely sliced
½ thumb-sized piece of ginger,
   cut into matchsticks
1 onion, finely sliced
3 tablespoons ready-made
   crispy fried onions
2 birds' eye chillies, pierced
   with the tip of your knife
600g (1lb 5oz) prepared squash
   or pumpkin, chopped into
   large chunks
400g (14oz) green beans,
   cut into 3–4cm (1¼–1½ inch)
   lengths
vegetable oil
steamed rice, to serve
lime wedges, to garnish

STOCK
400ml (14fl oz) coconut milk
200ml (7fl oz) vegetable stock
1½ teaspoons salt
½ teaspoon black pepper

Traditionally *ginataang kalabasa* would be made with pork and prawns to flavour the stew. However, the staple ingredient of this recipe is the squash, so I've kept this vegan to showcase its wonderful flavour and texture.

1. Stir the stock ingredients together in a jug.

2. **Build Your Wok Clock:** Start at 12 o'clock with the garlic, followed by the ginger, onion, crispy fried onions, chillies, squash, stock and lastly the green beans.

3. Heat 1 tablespoon of vegetable oil in your wok to a medium heat and add the garlic. Stir-fry for 30 seconds, then add the ginger and sliced onion and continue to stir-fry for a further 2 minutes. Add the crispy fried onions, chillies and the squash, fold through and stir-fry for 5–6 minutes.

4. Pour one-quarter of the stock into the wok and bring to a vigorous boil. Once boiling, add another quarter of the stock and return to the boil before pouring in the rest. Return to the boil and continue to cook for 10–15 minutes.

5. Once the squash is soft, push into 2–3 of the pieces with a ladle or spoon to mash it up and help thicken the sauce. Allow the stew to boil for a further 5 minutes before adding the green beans. Continue cooking for another 2–3 minutes to just soften the beans before serving. Serve over steamed fish with lime wedges on the side to garnish.

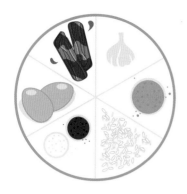

BREAKFAST-STYLE BEEF TAPA

PREP: 15 MINS, PLUS MARINATING | COOK: 10 MINS | SERVES 2

400g (14oz) sirloin steak,
    finely sliced against
    the grain
2 eggs
vegetable oil
½ cucumber, cut into
    bite-sized chunks
1 tomato, cut into
    bite-sized chunks

MARINADE
4 garlic cloves, finely sliced
2 tablespoons rice vinegar
2 tablespoons palm sugar
    (swapsies: soft brown sugar)
1½ tablespoons light soy sauce
½ teaspoon dark soy sauce
½ teaspoon black pepper

GARLIC RICE
3 garlic cloves, finely chopped
½ teaspoon ground turmeric
150g (5½oz) cooked white rice,
    at room temperature
salt and pepper

Breakfast in the Philippines usually includes some sort of marinated and fried meat, accompanied by garlic rice and topped with a fried egg. Believe it or not, there's an art to frying an egg to get that perfect oozing yolk while holding its crisp edge, and every Filipino breakfast chef will now want a Rosie Reynolds (our dedicated food stylist) by their side to achieve it. This is traditionally quite sweet but I've tweaked it here to accommodate my own savoury-leaning palate. A power breakfast to set you up for the day.

1. Place the meat in a mixing bowl, add the marinade ingredients and massage well into the meat. Set aside for 10–15 minutes.

2. **Build Your Wok Clock:** Start at 12 o'clock with the garlic rice ingredients (starting with the garlic, followed by the turmeric, cooked rice, salt and pepper), then the eggs and lastly the marinated beef.

3. To make the garlic rice, heat 1 tablespoon of vegetable oil in your wok over a high heat. Add the garlic and stir-fry for 30 seconds before adding the turmeric. Immediately add the cooked rice, breaking up any clumps of rice with a spoon or spatula. Stir-fry for 2–3 minutes until the rice turns a uniform yellow colour and the grains are well separated. Season with salt and pepper to taste and divide between 2 serving plates, making sure you get every last grain from the wok.

4. Now heat 1–2 tablespoons of oil in the wok over a medium heat and fry the eggs sunny side up until the whites are set. Once cooked, place one egg on top of each plate of rice.

5. Give the wok a quick clean with kitchen paper, then return to the hob and heat another 1–2 tablespoons of vegetable oil to a high heat. Place the marinated meat in the wok and press each piece down into the oil with your spatula to sear well for 30–60 seconds. Turn the meat and sear the other side for a further 30–60 seconds before stir-frying to finish for a further minute or so. Serve next to the fried rice along with cucumber and tomato chunks on the side.

KOREAN & JAPANESE

Both Korean and Japanese cuisines share a meticulous and methodical approach to their cooking techniques, which allows them to take simple ingredients and elevate them to showcase both flavour and texture. Take something as simple as a grain of rice, perfectly grown to a specific shape and roundness and then fastidiously cleaned or processed to a point where cooking with it yields such joyous results. Both cuisines take pride in such precision and respect for the ingredients – rice in particular – at hand.

When it comes to the Korean pantry, I'd recommend experimenting with different grains of rice and testing out any ready-made kimchi you can get hold of if you are just starting your fermented food journey. You should also definitely stock up on Korean chilli paste (*gochujang*), Korean chilli flakes (*gochugaru*) and toasted sesame seeds to give you some basic flavours from which to start.

Coming to the Japanese pantry, the soy sauces are slightly different to Chinese light and dark soy sauces as they are lighter, more subtle and less syrupy in texture, making them better for Japanese dipping sauces to complement the subtlety of the cuisine. Of course, if you'd rather not double up on soy sauces, then take your pick from the various cuisines – just so long as you understand the differences in flavour profiles and make sure you adjust accordingly in your cooking.

A note on texture: we have come full circle from the Chinese chapter in the discussion of balance. With both Japanese and Korean cuisines, a balance of flavours and textures is what creates harmony in a dish or a table full of dishes. Think of beautifully balanced bento boxes, tables full of teppanyaki ingredients or Korean barbecued meats surrounded with little plates of vegetable *namul*, kimchi, pickles and side dishes to touch every part of the palate – a little bit of everything is sure to whet and satisfy your palate and appetite!

My final word of advice on cooking the dishes in this chapter is to keep it simple and try not to do too much at one time, certainly not at first. Make every slice count and work on frying to perfection. Stand over the stove and make that roux for the katsu curry with nothing else on your mind. Bring a sense of calm and focus – a zen-like attitude if you will – to your cooking: your food and tastebuds will thank you for it.

KIMCHI FRIED RICE

PREP: 10 MINS | COOK: 11 MINS | SERVES 2

2 eggs, lightly beaten
½ thumb-sized piece of ginger,
    peeled and finely chopped
1–2 garlic cloves, finely chopped
100g (3½oz) kimchi,
    roughly chopped
handful of frozen peas
250–300g (9–10½oz) cooked
    Korean or jasmine rice,
    at room temperature
vegetable oil
1 spring onion, finely sliced
1 teaspoon sesame seeds

SAUCE
1 tablespoon *gochujang*
    (Korean chilli paste)
    (swapsies: chilli paste)
1 tablespoon kimchi liquid
    from the jar
½ tablespoon tomato ketchup
1 tablespoon light soy sauce
¼ teaspoon sugar
1 teaspoon sesame oil

If you are a rice fanatic (*faan tong* or 'rice bin' in Cantonese) like me, you'll know that changing the grain of rice from dish to dish can create a completely different texture and so a whole different meal. My preference here is to use Korean white rice as the grains tend to feel a little thicker, creating a unique texture and bite to the fried rice.

1. Mix the sauce ingredients together in a small bowl.

2. **Build Your Wok Clock:** Start at 12 o'clock with the beaten egg, followed by the ginger, garlic, kimchi, frozen peas, cooked rice and the sauce.

3. Heat 1 teaspoon of vegetable oil in your wok over a high heat. Once smoking hot, pour in the beaten egg and swirl around the wok. Stir-fry for 1–2 minutes until crispy at the edges but not burnt, then push aside. Next add your ginger and garlic, the kimchi, frozen peas and then the rice, stir-frying for 30 seconds before adding in each new ingredient. Once in the wok, separate the rice grains by pressing into any clumps with your spatula or ladle. Continue to cook through and mix for 3–4 minutes.

4. Pour the sauce evenly over the rice and stir-fry for a further 1–2 minutes. Once the rice has absorbed all the liquid, sprinkle with finely sliced spring onion and sesame seeds and serve.

BULGOGI

PREP: 15 MINS, PLUS MARINATING | COOK: 17 MINS | SERVES 2

300–400g (10½–14oz)
    rib-eye steak
vegetable oil
2–3 spring onions,
    halved lengthways
2 Little Gem lettuces,
    halved lengthways

MARINADE
1 ripe pear, cored
4 tablespoons light soy sauce
2 tablespoons palm sugar
    (swapsies: soft brown sugar)
2 garlic cloves, finely chopped
½ thumb-sized piece of ginger,
    peeled and finely chopped
2 spring onions, finely chopped
1 tablespoon sesame seeds
1 tablespoon sesame oil
salt and pepper

BARBECUE SAUCE
    (SSAMJANG)
2 tablespoons *gochujang*
    (Korean chilli paste)
    (swapsies: chilli paste)
1 tablespoon miso paste
½ tablespoon light soy sauce
1 tablespoon honey
1 teaspoon sesame oil
1 tablespoon toasted
    sesame seeds

Despite spending only 24 hours in Seoul on a stopover to visit my long-lost Korean Auntie, I can recall eating bulgogi six times while I was there, all between meals! It was my and my sister's way of seizing every opportunity we had, from the moment we stepped onto the Korean Air flight. The love of both eating and feeding others is a family trait that cannot be contained within borders, especially when the food is this good!

1. Slice the steak as finely as possible against the grain in long, wide pieces, then bash well with the side of your knife, cleaver or meat mallet to flatten them out. Blitz the marinade ingredients in a food processor until smooth, then pour over the meat and massage well. Cover and set aside for 30 minutes, or chill in the fridge overnight.

2. Mix the *ssamjang* ingredients together in a bowl. When you are ready to cook, rub 1 tablespoon of vegetable oil over the cut sides of the spring onions and lettuces.

3. Heat your wok over a high heat. Once hot, place the cut sides of the lettuce halves and spring onions directly onto the dry wok to char for 1–2 minutes, then transfer to a plate. Heat 2–3 tablespoons of vegetable oil in the wok, still over a high heat. Once smoking hot, place a few pieces of marinated meat, piece by piece, into the wok and sear until nicely charred – 2–3 minutes on each side. Transfer to the plate with the charred vegetables and repeat with another batch of meat until it has all been cooked. Serve the meat and charred veg with the *ssamjang* on the side for dipping.

KOREAN FRIED CHICKEN

PREP: 12 MINS | COOK: 12 MINS | SERVES 2

4–5 large dried red chillies
8 chicken wings
handful of toasted peanuts
4–5 garlic cloves, finely sliced
vegetable oil
1 tablespoon sesame seeds,
    to garnish

SAUCE
1 teaspoon English mustard
2 tablespoons *gochujang*
    (Korean chilli paste)
    (swapsies: chilli paste)
2 tablespoons light soy sauce
3 tablespoons maple syrup
    or honey
1 tablespoon palm sugar
    (swapsies: soft brown sugar)
1 tablespoon rice vinegar

MARINADE
½ teaspoon sea salt flakes
½ teaspoon black pepper
½ thumb-sized piece of ginger,
    peeled and finely chopped
2 garlic cloves, finely chopped
200g (7oz) cornflour
1 teaspoon baking powder

What a lucky name for a dish – it just naturally gets abbreviated to the same initials as one of the most famous fast food chains. But make no mistake, this dish is far superior and perhaps much better placed to take over the world.

1. Soak the dried red chillies in hot water for 10 minutes, then drain and roughly chop. Mix the sauce ingredients together in a small bowl until the sugar fully dissolves.

2. Slice through the joints of the chicken wings to separate the flats and drums, making them easier to fry without using excessive amounts of oil. Place the pieces in a large mixing bowl and massage the marinade ingredients well into the meat, taking care to add the cornflour and baking powder at the end.

3. **Build Your Wok Clock:** Start at 12 o'clock with the bowl of marinated chicken wings, followed by the peanuts, garlic, chopped dried chillies and lastly the sauce.

4. Deep-fry the coated chicken in vegetable oil at 180°C (350°F) for 1 minute (see page 21), before reducing the heat to medium. Continue to deep-fry for 6–8 minutes, turning the chicken wings occasionally, until very crisp and golden brown. Transfer the chicken to a plate lined with kitchen paper.

5. If using your wok for deep-frying, carefully pour out the oil into a heatproof bowl to cool and give your wok a quick wipe with kitchen paper. Place the wok back on the hob and bring 2 tablespoons of vegetable oil to a medium heat. Stir-fry the peanuts for 30 seconds before adding the garlic. Then add the dried chillies, stir-fry for 30 seconds, increase the heat to high and pour in the sauce. Bring to a boil and reduce the sauce by half, until thickened to a light syrupy texture – 1–2 minutes. Add the fried chicken into the wok and fold through until fully coated with sauce. Garnish with the sesame seeds and serve.

Rice Vinager

Palm Sugar

Maple Syrup

English Mustard

Light Soy Sauce

Korean Chilli Paste

CHICKEN WINGS

SAUCE

PEANUTS

CHILLIES

GARLIC

100g (3½oz) plain flour,
  seasoned with a good pinch
  of salt and pepper
1 egg, lightly beaten
10 tablespoons mixed black and
  white sesame seeds
2 skin-on salmon fillets, descaled
½ thumb-sized piece of ginger,
  peeled and cut into matchsticks
2 spring onions, trimmed and
  halved lengthways
vegetable oil

SAUCE

1 tablespoon light soy sauce
2 tablespoons dark soy sauce
2 tablespoons mirin
1 tablespoon honey

TERIYAKI SESAME SALMON

PREP: 10 MINS | COOK: 8 MINS | SERVES 2

This one is thanks to my wife: it was the first 'posh meal' I cooked for her almost 20 years ago and look where it got us! Understanding her palate now, I'm certain it's the crunchy sesame seed crust that won her over. It's simple, yet super-satisfying to make and eat.

1. Mix the sauce ingredients together in a small bowl. Spread the flour onto a tray or plate and season well. Place the beaten egg in a shallow bowl and the sesame seeds in another.

2. Pat the salmon dry with kitchen paper, then dip the skin side into the flour to fully cover the skin. Next dip the skin side into the egg, then press it down into the sesame seeds so that they stick well. Repeat with the other fillet of salmon, leaving the flesh sides of the fish uncoated.

3. **Build Your Wok Clock:** Start at 12 o'clock with the coated salmon, followed by the ginger, spring onions and the sauce.

4. Heat 2–3 tablespoons of vegetable oil in your wok over a high heat and carefully place the salmon fillets skin-side down into the oil, gently pressing them down with a spatula. Sear for 1 minute, then reduce the heat to medium and cook for 3–4 minutes or until the bottom half of the flesh turns a light pink.

5. Scatter the ginger and spring onions around the fillets of salmon and increase the heat to high before flipping the salmon over. Sear for another minute, then pour the sauce around the sides of the salmon, avoiding the crust to keep it crispy. Bring to a vigorous boil for 2 minutes and serve crusted side up.

CHICKEN KATSU CURRY

PREP: 15 MINS | COOK: 25 MINS | SERVES 2

2 skinless, boneless
    chicken breasts
2 tablespoons unsalted butter
2 tablespoons plain flour
500ml (18fl oz) chicken stock
vegetable oil

BATTER STATION
100g (3½oz) plain flour
½ teaspoon medium
    curry powder
1 teaspoon salt
1 teaspoon pepper
2 eggs, well beaten
200g (7oz) panko breadcrumbs

SPICE PASTE
1 tablespoon medium
    curry powder
1 teaspoon garam masala
½ teaspoon paprika
1½ tablespoons light soy sauce
1 tablespoon mirin
½ tablespoon honey
6-8 tablespoons chicken stock

TO SERVE
steamed rice
handful of mixed leafy salad
1 tablespoon pickled ginger

Katsu's combination of base curry spices and the 'French style' roux, along with the crispy panko are what create a perfectly balanced dish. It's this balance of flavours and textures that makes it so moreish and popular.

1. Butterfly the chicken breasts by slicing horizontally most of the way through the middle and opening them up like a book. Place between 2 sheets of baking paper and bash with a rolling pin to tenderize the meat and thin out to roughly 1cm (½ inch).

2. Prepare the batter station by mixing the flour, curry powder, salt and pepper in a shallow bowl, placing the eggs in another and the breadcrumbs in a third. Dip the chicken in the seasoned flour until well coated, shake off any excess, then dip into the egg, making sure the chicken is coated on both sides. Let any excess egg drip off before dipping the chicken into the breadcrumbs, covering the meat completely.

3. Mix the spice paste ingredients together in a small bowl.

4. **Build Your Wok Clock:** Start at 12 o'clock with the butter, then follow with the flour, spice paste and the chicken stock.

5. Melt the butter in your wok over a low heat. When it starts to bubble and fizz, add the flour. Mix well to form a smooth roux. Add the spice paste, 2 tablespoons at a time, stirring constantly and allowing the paste to bubble up in between each addition. Once you have formed a smooth, thin paste your spiced roux is ready. Now pour the chicken stock in, stir and bring to the boil. Reduce the heat to a simmer, cover with a lid and cook for 15-20 minutes. Remove the lid and continue to cook the sauce to your desired consistency.

6. While the curry sauce is cooking, deep-fry the coated chicken in vegetable oil at 180°C (350°F) for 6-7 minutes until golden brown (see page 21). Alternatively, shallow-fry the chicken in a frying pan. Transfer the cooked chicken to a plate lined with kitchen paper, then chop into slices. Serve the chicken smothered in curry sauce over a bed of steamed rice with the leafy salad and pickled ginger on the side.

BUTTER

CHICKEN STOCK

FLOUR

SPICE PASTE

STEAMED SESAME AUBERGINE

PREP: 5 MINS | COOK: 14 MINS | SERVES 2

2-3 aubergines, cut into
2cm (¾ inch) thick pieces

DRESSING
3 garlic cloves, finely chopped
2 spring onions, chopped
1 tablespoon light soy sauce
1 teaspoon fish sauce
1 teaspoon Korean chilli flakes
or other chilli flakes
2 teaspoons sesame oil
1 tablespoon toasted
sesame seeds

Sometimes side dishes and appetizers are so tasty I feel like they would be better as main courses. This is one of them. Perfect for a quick mid-week meal with rice on the side, and perhaps a fried egg on top.

1. Place the aubergine pieces in a large shallow heatproof bowl and steam for 8-10 minutes (see page 20). Mix the dressing ingredients together in a bowl.

2. When the aubergine is tender and fully cooked, remove the lid, pour the dressing over the aubergine, cover again and steam for a further 3-4 minutes. Serve.

JAPCHAE

PREP: 20 MINS, PLUS SOAKING | COOK: 9 MINS | SERVES 2

150g (5½oz) sweet
   potato vermicelli
150g (5½oz) rib-eye steak or
   minute steak, finely sliced
   into 3mm (⅛ inch) strips
1 egg
1 garlic clove, finely sliced
1 small red onion, sliced
1 carrot, peeled and cut
   into matchsticks
½ red pepper, finely sliced
4 shiitake mushrooms,
   finely sliced
handful of spinach
vegetable oil
toasted sesame seeds,
   to garnish

MARINADE
1 garlic clove, finely chopped
1 tablespoon light soy sauce
1 tablespoon mirin
½ teaspoon black pepper
1 teaspoon sesame oil

SAUCE
2 tablespoons light soy sauce
1 teaspoon palm sugar
   (swapsies: soft brown sugar)
1 tablespoon oyster sauce
100ml (3½fl oz) chicken stock
1 teaspoon sesame oil

Traditionally, each ingredient in *japchae* (stir-fried glass noodles) is cooked separately, then mixed at the end due to the different cooking times of all the ingredients. Here, you can let the Wok Clock do the work – adding one ingredient to the wok at a time ensures they all get the correct cooking time, avoiding too much extra faff and still achieving great results!

1. Soak the noodles in hot water for 10 minutes until tender, then drain and refresh in cold water. Mix the marinade ingredients in a mixing bowl, add the meat and massage the marinade into the meat. Mix the sauce ingredients together in a bowl.

2. **Build Your Wok Clock:** Start at 12 o'clock with the egg, followed by the sliced garlic, red onion, carrot, red pepper, mushrooms, spinach, marinated meat, noodles and lastly the sauce.

3. Heat 1 tablespoon of vegetable oil in your wok to a medium-high heat. Once smoking hot, crack the egg into the wok and fold through, breaking the yolk only when the white is halfway cooked, to keep the white and yolk separate from each other. Push the egg to the back of the wok, then add the garlic and red onion and stir-fry for 30 seconds. Next add the carrot, red pepper, mushrooms and spinach, stir-frying for 30 seconds before adding in each new ingredient. Transfer the vegetables to a bowl.

4. Heat 1 tablespoon of vegetable oil in the wok over a high heat. Once smoking hot, add the marinated meat and stir-fry for 1 minute. Return the vegetables to the wok, then add the noodles and continue to stir-fry for 1 minute. Add the sauce, bring to a vigorous boil and stir-fry for 2–3 minutes until all the sauce has been absorbed by the noodles. Serve sprinkled with toasted sesame seeds.

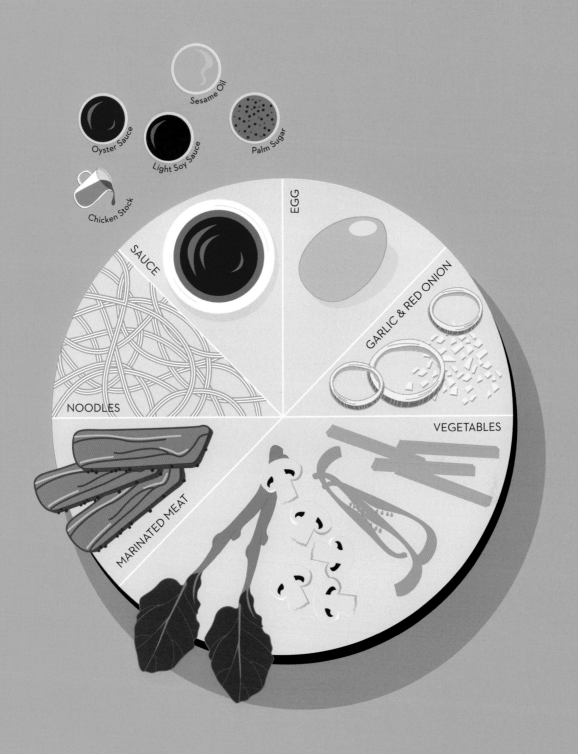

Oyster Sauce

Sesame Oil

Light Soy Sauce

Palm Sugar

Chicken Stock

SAUCE

EGG

GARLIC & RED ONION

NOODLES

VEGETABLES

MARINATED MEAT

MIXED VEGGIE TEMPURA

PREP: 16 MINS | COOK: 32 MINS | SERVES 2

A medley of vegetables covered in a light tempura batter works so well. It's the variety of textures and flavours from the different vegetables that keeps you going back for more, even though it's all coated in the same batter.

100g (3½oz) Tenderstem broccoli spears
1 aubergine, sliced diagonally into 5mm (¼ inch) slices
1 sweet potato, unpeeled, sliced into 3mm (⅛ inch) slices
bunch of asparagus spears, halved lengthways
10 oyster mushrooms, roughly torn
10 shiso leaves (optional)
vegetable oil

DIPPING SAUCE
50–100g (1¾–3½oz) white radish or daikon (optional)
½ thumb-sized piece of ginger, cut into matchsticks
1 tablespoon mirin
2 tablespoons light soy sauce
1 tablespoon rice vinegar

TEMPURA BATTER
10 tablespoons plain flour
2 tablespoons cornflour
130–140ml (4–4½fl oz) chilled sparkling water
½ teaspoon salt
½ teaspoon black pepper

1. Grate the radish for the dipping sauce, if using, and place in a bowl. Cover with a sheet of damp kitchen paper and chill in the fridge until ready to serve. Mix the rest of the dipping sauce ingredients together in a separate bowl.

2. Mix the batter ingredients together in a large mixing bowl ready for frying. One at a time, dip the vegetables into the batter and deep-fry in vegetable oil at 180°C (350°F) for 3–4 minutes until golden brown (see page 21). Cook the vegetables in batches of 6–8 pieces, adding them to the oil individually, so the oil retains its heat. During cooking, dip a fork or chopsticks into the bowl of batter and carefully scatter a little over the top of the frying tempura to create a bubbly frill of batter over each vegetable. When crisp and golden brown, transfer the vegetables to a plate lined with kitchen paper and keep warm (see page 21). Repeat until all the vegetables are cooked. Pour the dipping sauce over the grated daikon and serve on the side.

QUICK VEGAN RAMEN

PREP: 20 MINS | COOK: 45 MINS | SERVES 2

1 small onion,
  unpeeled, quartered
1 thumb-sized piece of ginger,
  cut into matchsticks
5 garlic cloves,
  unpeeled, bashed
4 spring onions,
  roughly chopped
6–8 shiitake mushrooms,
  roughly torn
1.5–2 litres (2¾–3½ pints)
  vegetable stock
1 heaped teaspoon white
  miso paste
1 tablespoon light soy sauce
200g (7oz) fresh ramen noodles
1 head of pak choi,
  quartered lengthways
vegetable oil

MISO GLAZE
1 tablespoon red miso paste
1 tablespoon maple syrup
1 tablespoon light soy sauce
1 teaspoon rice vinegar
1 teaspoon sesame oil
2 tablespoons water

TO BE GLAZED
200g (7oz) firm tofu,
  cut into batons
2 small carrots,
  quartered lengthways
1 spring onion,
  halved lengthways

Although ramen is traditionally served with a soy-marinated egg on top, this recipe is for our lovely vegan videographer Chris, whose animation skills are second to none. If you want to add the classic soft-boiled egg, add 15–20 tablespoons of dark soy sauce to a pan of boiling water and cook room-temperature eggs for 6 minutes. Cool in iced water, peel and leave in the cooled soy liquid until ready to serve.

1. Mix the miso glaze ingredients together in a small bowl.

2. **Build Your Wok Clock:** Start at 12 o'clock with the onion, followed by the ginger, garlic, chopped spring onions, shiitake mushrooms, vegetable stock, white miso paste, light soy sauce, ramen noodles and lastly the pak choi.

3. Heat 1 tablespoon of oil in your wok to a medium heat and add the onion, ginger, garlic, spring onions and shiitake mushrooms, stir-frying for 30 seconds between each addition. Add the stock, white miso paste and light soy sauce and bring to the boil. Reduce the heat and simmer for 30–45 minutes.

4. Meanwhile, heat 1 tablespoon of oil in a frying pan over a medium heat. Place the tofu into the middle of the pan and the carrot quarters around the edges. Fry, turning from time to time, until the tofu is browned on both sides. Now add the spring onion around the edge of the pan and continue to fry for 1–2 minutes. Pour the miso glaze over the top of it all and bring to a vigorous boil for 2–3 minutes until syrupy in texture.

5. Remove the stock from the heat and sieve into a large bowl. Discard all the flavouring ingredients except for the shiitake mushrooms. Pour the stock and mushrooms back into the wok over a medium heat, bring to the boil and add the ramen noodles. Cook for approximately 2 minutes before transferring them to your serving bowls. Next, add the pak choi to the stock, boil for 30–60 seconds then place on top of the noodles. Top with the glazed tofu, carrots and spring onion before ladling the stock over the bowls to fully cover the vegetables.

YASAI YAKI UDON

PREP: 15 MINS | COOK: 6 MINS | SERVES 2

200–300g (7–10½oz) fresh
    udon noodles
1 teaspoon sesame oil
2 garlic cloves, finely sliced
2 spring onions, cut into
    3–4cm (1¼–1½ inch) chunks
1 carrot, cut into matchsticks
½ red pepper, finely sliced
100g (3½oz) pak choi,
    roughly chopped
    (swapsies: cavolo nero)
6–8 shiitake mushrooms,
    roughly torn
vegetable oil
1 tablespoon shredded pink
    pickled ginger, to garnish

SAUCE
1 tablespoon light soy sauce
½ tablespoon oyster sauce
    (swapsies: vegetarian
    stir-fry sauce)
1 tablespoon mirin or rice wine
2 tablespoons dark soy sauce
1 teaspoon palm sugar
    (swapsies: soft brown sugar)

When my dad was around, evenings of garden teppanyaki (griddle cooking) were a treat to remember. Interactive cooking is a core part of many Asian cuisines and my dad was adamant that there was a skill to be learned in piling the table high with a colourful array of prepped ingredients for us all to cook together. He always stressed the importance of knowing in what order to cook the ingredients to utilize all the juices or flavours lingering on the griddle top. Yaki udon (fried noodles) always came last with every teppanyaki cooking adventure, as the noodles were perfect for mopping up any charred bits of spring onion or garlic butter that we might have missed from the seafood round.

1. Soak the noodles in hot water for 1 minute until tender, then drain and refresh in cold water. Place in a bowl and mix the sesame oil into the noodles to avoid sticking. Mix the sauce ingredients together in a bowl until the sugar fully dissolves.

2. **Build Your Wok Clock:** Start at 12 o'clock with the garlic and spring onions, followed by the carrot, red pepper, pak choi, mushrooms, noodles and lastly the sauce.

3. Heat 1 tablespoon of vegetable oil in your wok to a high heat. Once smoking hot, add the garlic and spring onions, followed by the carrot, red pepper, pack choi and mushrooms, stir-frying for 30 seconds between each addition. Add the noodles to the wok and stir-fry for a further minute.

4. Make sure the wok is smoking hot once again, then pour the sauce in and bring to a vigorous boil. Give your wok a vigorous shake while stirring with your ladle or spatula (like a 'tummy and head' movement, see page 19) to distribute the sauce evenly throughout the noodles. Continue to stir-fry for 1–2 minutes until the sauce evenly coats all the ingredients. Serve immediately, garnished with the pickled ginger.

TASTY SIDES

These side dishes are here to provide a balance of flavour, colour and texture across the table, filling in those gaps and lightening and brightening the delicious recipes you have now learned to cook. No Asian meal, no matter which cuisine you're cooking, is complete without a good bowl of rice or some vibrant salads and bright green vegetables on the side.

These recipes are all incredibly easy to make, whether it's a sweet and sour egg dish to add some excitement to a mid-week meal, or a selection of Korean *namul* (seasoned vegetable dishes) to balance out your barbecued meats or Korean fried chicken. The Malaysian and Thai salads and chilli sauces can be served alongside any of the main recipes in any of the chapters. There are also recipes for some Chinese *liang ban*, which can be translated literally as 'cold vegetarian dishes dressed with sauce' (or Chinese salads, for those who would accept the term, although it's not really used within the culture). These provide the yin to the yang and go particularly well with fatty meats and deep-fried foods.

I highly recommend trying out any of these dishes to accompany the main dishes in the book, no matter which cuisine. These sides have been chosen to work together however you wish, to fill those gaps, entice palates and appetites and encourage you to keep cooking and keep sharing your food with those you love, enjoying the process along the way.

STEAMED RICE

There are many different types of rice grain in the world. I feel like the simplest way to decipher how to cook each grain is to consider how processed the grains are and whether the husk has been left on or milled off. White rice, for example, has had the outer husk of the grain removed and a milling of the bran layer or membrane, which is left unprocessed on grains such as brown rice. As a general rule, the more processed rice takes less time to cook, needs less water and is less likely to need any soaking before cooking.

When cooking rice, the same method of washing and steaming works well whatever grain you are using. I always use a cup to measure the rice and liquid; you don't need a specific type of cup, anything that holds rice will do. Whatever you use – whether it's an American cup measure, a rice cup or just a mug or small tumbler you have in your cupboard – so long as you stay true to the suggested ratio of rice to liquid, the method will work. The cup I use is 240ml (8½fl oz) and holds 195g (6½oz) of rice. I use 1 cup of rice for 2 people, or 2 cups for 4 people.

No matter what grain you use, you must wash the rice at least three times before cooking to remove the starch, if not five or six times. Don't wash it four times – in Chinese tradition, we don't do things by fours as it's unlucky! When washing, place the rice in a bowl and run under cold water, gently moving the rice grains between the tips of your fingers. The excess starch from the rice grains will initially make the water quite cloudy, so pour the rice through a sieve between each wash. By the end of the washing process, the water should run clear.

To cook the rice, soak it first if required (see recipes opposite) then place in a saucepan with the correct amount of liquid following the ratios suggested. Cover with a tight-fitting lid, place on the hob over a medium-high heat and bring to a vigorous boil. Once boiling, reduce the heat to low and simmer with the lid on for 12–15 minutes until the liquid has evaporated to the point where you start to see air pockets form between some of the rice grains. Replace the lid, turn the heat off and leave the rice for a further 15 minutes.

JASMINE RICE

(Ratio of liquid to rice 1:1)
1 cup rice
1 cup water

Cook the rice following
the method opposite.

COCONUT RICE

(Ratio of liquid to rice 1:1)
1 cup jasmine rice
1/2 cup coconut water
1/2 cup chicken or vegetable stock
1/2 teaspoon sugar
1–2 pandan leaves, tied into knots (optional)
pinch of salt

Place all the ingredients in the
pan and cook the rice following
the method opposite.

KOREAN PURPLE RICE

(Ratio of liquid to rice 1¼:1)
1 cup short-grain Korean white rice
1 tablespoon Korean black rice (purple rice)
1¼ cups water

Soak the rice in cold water for
30 minutes, then cook following
the method opposite.

JAPANESE RICE WITH SEAWEED SEASONING

(Ratio of liquid to rice 1¼:1)
1 cup rice
1¼ cups water
1 tablespoon dried, shredded nori
1 tablespoon sesame seeds

Soak the rice in cold water for
30 minutes, then cook following
the method opposite. Sprinkle
with the nori and sesame seeds
before serving.

BROWN RICE

(Ratio of liquid to rice 1½:1)
1 cup brown rice
1½ cups water
1 tablespoon unsalted butter
small handful of finely chopped dill

Soak the rice in cold water for
45 minutes, then cook following
the method opposite. Fold the
butter and dill into the rice just
before serving.

HOMEMADE SAMBAL

PREP: 10 MINS, PLUS SOAKING
COOK: 20 MINS | MAKES 300ML (10FL OZ)

10 dried chillies
10 large red chillies,
   finely chopped
2 red onions, finely chopped
2 lemon grass stalks, trimmed,
   bruised and finely chopped
1 thumb-sized piece of galangal
   or ginger, peeled and
   finely chopped
6 garlic cloves, finely chopped
6 candlenuts or macadamia
   nuts (optional)
1–2 teaspoons *belacan*
   (toasted shrimp paste) or
   2 teaspoons ready-made
   crispy fried onions
vegetable oil

SAMBAL LIQUID
1 tablespoon tomato purée
3 tablespoons tamarind
   concentrate
3 tablespoons light soy sauce
6 tablespoons kecap manis
   (sweet soy sauce)
1 teaspoon salt
8 tablespoons water

When I cook this sambal I seem to send my in-laws into the equivalent of a 1970s Tupperware party frenzy. If I were so inclined, I'm pretty sure I could start a bidding war for who gets to take home the biggest jar, to be snuck into a secret stash at the back of the fridge, its presence unknown to other family members. It's just that good. It's great on the side as an accompaniment, or as a base for many recipes. It can even be used as the main driving force of flavour for several dishes. Or take my in-laws' advice and eat it with scrambled eggs, toasted sandwiches, or just spooned out of the jar on its own.

1. Soak the dried red chillies in hot water for 10 minutes, then drain and finely chop. Mix the sambal liquid ingredients together in a bowl. Pound all the remaining ingredients (except the vegetable oil) using a pestle and mortar or blend together in a food processor until you have a smooth paste.

2. Heat 5–6 tablespoons of vegetable oil in a wok over a medium heat, then add the paste. Reduce the heat to low and fry for 8–10 minutes until the paste turns a dark orange or brown colour. Now add the liquid ingredients, stir through, increase the heat to medium and bring to the boil. Reduce the heat once again to low and simmer for 4–5 minutes.

3. Continue cooking until the sambal stops steaming and starts to sizzle again, signifying a reduction in liquid. Keep scraping the bottom of the wok every so often to create a 'chilli jam' underneath the oil. Transfer to a sterilized jar, seal the jar and allow to cool. Store in the fridge for up to a week if your family allow it to last that long.

NAM JIM JAEW

PREP: 10 MINS | COOK: 7 MINS | MAKES 150ML (5FL OZ)

1 tablespoon dry jasmine rice
5 dried red chillies
½ red onion, finely sliced
1 spring onion, finely sliced
small handful of coriander
   leaves

SAUCE
2 tablespoons fish sauce
1 tablespoon palm sugar
   (swapsies: soft brown sugar)
juice of ½ lime

Nam jim jaew **is an extremely versatile, savoury spicy sauce which can sit on the side of any Thai dish. It's especially tasty with grilled pork or deep-fried foods, but equally as great poured over a plate of fried rice or noodles.**

1. Toast the rice grains in a dry wok on a medium heat for 4-5 minutes until uniformly golden brown. Allow to cool, then grind the grains to a powder using a pestle and mortar or spice grinder. Toast the dried chillies in the same way for 1-2 minutes until fragrant, then grind to a fine powder.

2. Place the red onion, spring onion and coriander in a bowl and add the ground chillies. Add the sauce ingredients and mix together until all the palm sugar has dissolved. Sprinkle the toasted rice powder over the top to finish the sauce and serve.

GARLIC PEA SHOOTS

PREP: 5 MINS | COOK: 2 MINS | SERVES 1–2

vegetable oil
4–5 garlic cloves, finely chopped
300g (10½oz) pea shoots

SAUCE
½ tablespoon light soy sauce
½ tablespoon Shaoxing rice
    wine (swapsies: dry sherry)
pinch of sea salt flakes

In many Chinese restaurants, you can (and should!) ask the waiting staff what fresh green vegetables are being served that day. Pea shoots, whenever available, are definitely my favourite; they usually come stir-fried in garlic or blanched with oyster sauce on the side.

1. Mix the sauce ingredients together in a bowl.

2. Heat 1 tablespoon of vegetable oil in a wok over a high heat. Once smoking hot, add the garlic and stir-fry for 30 seconds. Then add the pea shoots and flash-fry for 30 seconds before pouring the sauce into the wok. Fold through 2–3 times to evenly coat the shoots and serve.

SPINACH GOMA AE

PREP: 5 MINS | COOK: 1 MIN | SERVES 1–2

400g (14oz) spinach leaves
1 tablespoon toasted
    sesame seeds

DRESSING
1½ tablespoons sesame sauce
    (swapsies: tahini)
1 tablespoon light soy sauce
1 tablespoon mirin
1 tablespoon rice vinegar
1 teaspoon sesame oil

My sister went through a phase of adding Japanese sesame dressing to everything she cooked. I don't blame her, it's so tasty. The spinach soaks up the dressing really quickly, making it simple and so moreish.

1. Mix the dressing ingredients together in a small bowl.

2. Half-fill your wok with water and bring to a boil; blanch the spinach leaves for 30 seconds. Drain through a sieve, then transfer the spinach to a bowl of cold water for 1–2 minutes to cool. Drain again and gently squeeze the spinach to remove any excess water. Place in a serving bowl then toss the dressing and toasted sesame seeds through the spinach using tongs or spoons and serve.

MIXED KOREAN SIDES

PREP: 15 MINS | COOK: 2 MINS | SERVES 1–2

2 spring onions,
   cut into matchsticks
½ cucumber, sliced
salt
1 courgette, finely sliced
toasted sesame seeds
sesame oil
3–4 handfuls of
   beansprouts, rinsed
4–5 tablespoons kimchi

CHILLI DRESSING
¼ teaspoon sugar
1 tablespoon *gochugaru*
   (Korean chilli flakes)
1 spring onion, sliced
1 garlic clove, finely chopped
1 teaspoon rice vinegar
1 teaspoon sesame oil
1 tablespoon toasted
   sesame seeds

Korean side dish options are plentiful, with flavours so vibrant and colourful they brighten up just about any meal. I highly encourage you to cook any or all of these *namul* (seasoned vegetable dishes) alongside the main Korean dishes from this book.

1. Place the spring onion matchsticks into a bowl of ice-cold water for 10 minutes to allow them to curl. Mix the chilli dressing ingredients together in a small bowl. Once the onions have curled, drain well through a sieve and place in a small serving bowl. Stir in 1–2 teaspoons of the chilli dressing.

2. Place the cucumber in a serving bowl, rub ½ teaspoon of salt into the slices and leave for 15 minutes. Rinse under cold water, drain well and return to the bowl. Add the rest of the chilli dressing and massage it well into the cucumber.

Half-fill your wok with water and bring to a boil; blanch the courgette slices for 1 minute. Remove with a slotted spoon and transfer to a small serving bowl. Season with sesame seeds, a drizzle of sesame oil and a pinch of salt. Blanch the beansprouts in the boiling water for 30 seconds then transfer to another bowl and season with sesame seeds, oil and salt. Place the kimchi in a separate serving bowl and let everyone help themselves.

HONG KONG TOMATO EGG

PREP: 5 MINS | COOK: 5 MINS | SERVES 2

½ red onion, finely sliced
1 spring onion, roughly chopped
1 large, ripe vine tomato,
    cut into 8 wedges
vegetable oil
handful of coriander leaves,
    to garnish

EGG MIXTURE
3 large eggs
½ tablespoon light soy sauce
1 teaspoon sesame oil

SAUCE
2 tablespoons tomato ketchup
1 tablespoon light soy sauce
1 tablespoon dark soy sauce
1½ tablespoons white
    wine vinegar
1½ tablespoons caster sugar

We have numerous 'special egg dishes' in our family, and this is a go-to for a quick hit of sweet and sour, without any hassle. It's so easy to make and the perfect accompaniment to a bowl of rice, some steamed fish or chicken and a side of stir-fried greens.

1. Beat the egg mixture ingredients together well in a bowl. Mix all the sauce ingredients together in a separate bowl.

2. **Build Your Wok Clock:** Start at 12 o'clock with the egg mixture, followed by the red onion, spring onion, tomato and lastly the sauce.

3. Heat 2 tablespoons of vegetable oil in your wok to a high heat. Once smoking hot, pour the egg mixture into the oil and swirl around the wok, then start to fold the egg into the wok and stir-fry for 1–2 minutes. Once the egg is half-cooked, tip onto a plate and return the wok to the heat.

4. Add ½ tablespoon of vegetable oil to the wok and once smoking hot, add the red onion, spring onion and tomato wedges, stir-frying for 30 seconds between each additional ingredient. Then tip the half-cooked egg back into the wok and immediately pour in the sauce and bring to a vigorous boil. Fold the sauce through the ingredients to coat evenly, then serve scattered with coriander leaves.

CHILLED SILKEN TOFU SALAD

PREP: 5 MINS | SERVES 2

400g (14oz) silken tofu,
   cut into bite-sized cubes
handful of coriander leaves,
   to garnish

DRESSING
3 garlic cloves, finely chopped
1 spring onion, finely sliced
1 tablespoon chilli bean sauce
   (*toban jiang*)
2 tablespoons light soy sauce
½ teaspoon sugar
1 teaspoon sesame oil

My dad taught me quite early on in life that you can always make something out of nothing. 'That's why coats have two pockets,' he used to say – one pocket for a bulb of garlic and the other for a tiny bottle of soy sauce and some chilli. That way, your next meal is only ever as far away as your jacket pockets. This no-cook tofu dish has so much flavour from so few ingredients and can be eaten cold as a side or spooned over a bowl of steaming hot rice.

1. Mix the dressing ingredients together in a bowl until the sugar dissolves.

2. Place the tofu on a serving dish, pour the dressing over the top and serve sprinkled with the coriander.

1 large cucumber, peeled,
    deseeded and thickly
    sliced diagonally
½ teaspoon sea salt flakes
50g (2oz) dried shrimp
    (optional)
1 ripe mango, peeled and
    thickly sliced diagonally

DRESSING
1 shallot, halved
    and finely sliced
1 tablespoon sambal,
    ready-made or homemade
    (see page 188)
juice of ½ lime
½ teaspoon sea salt flakes
1 teaspoon sugar

KERABU

PREP: 10 MINS, PLUS SALTING AND SOAKING | SERVES 2

This Malaysian salad is salty, spicy, sweet and sour and so simple to make. The chilli and lime in it add zing, while the mango provides a natural sweetness. This is a refreshing side to any meal.

1. Place the cucumber in a bowl, rub the salt into the slices and leave for 15 minutes. Rinse under cold water and drain well.

2. Soak the dried shrimps in a bowl of boiling water for 5 minutes. Drain and pound using a pestle and mortar until all the shrimps are smashed up.

3. Mix the dressing ingredients together in a large bowl, then add the cucumber, mango and dried shrimp and toss through to coat. Serve.

½ green apple, cut into chunks
2 handfuls of cubed pineapple
1 green mango, peeled and
    cut into chunks
½ cucumber, cut into chunks
vegetable oil (optional)
100g (3½oz) deep-fried
    tofu pieces (tofu pok),
    halved (optional)
handful of salted roasted
    peanuts, crushed
2 tablespoons toasted
    sesame seeds

DRESSING
1 tablespoon sambal, ready-made
    or homemade (see page 188)
1 tablespoon palm sugar
    (swapsies: soft brown sugar)
1 tablespoon hoisin sauce
1 tablespoon tamarind concentrate
½ tablespoon kecap manis
    (sweet soy sauce)
½ teaspoon sea salt flakes
1 teaspoon chilli powder
juice of ½ lime

ROJAK SALAD

PREP: 15 MINS | COOK: 3 MINS (OPTIONAL) | SERVES 2

Many cultures around the world pair local fruits with the heat of chilli and other savoury flavours. In Malaysia, this salad is a great example, and a fantastic use of the juicy tropical fruits grown there.

1. Mix the dressing ingredients together in a mixing bowl (reserving 1–2 tablespoons if using the tofu), add the fruit and veg and toss through.

2. If using the deep-fried tofu, heat ½ tablespoon of vegetable oil in your wok over a medium heat and add the tofu. Then add 1–2 tablespoons of the dressing and 2–3 tablespoons of water and boil for 2–3 minutes. Add the cooked tofu to the dressed salad, toss through and scatter with the peanuts and sesame seeds before serving.

GREEN PAPAYA SALAD

PREP: 20 MINS | COOK: 3 MINS | SERVES 2

100g (3½oz) green
   beans, trimmed
2 garlic cloves, finely sliced
2–3 birds' eye chillies, pierced
   with the tip of your knife
3 tablespoons dried shrimp
   (optional)
100g (3½oz) cherry
   tomatoes, quartered
½ aubergine, finely sliced
1 green papaya or green mango,
   cut into matchsticks (swapsies:
   1 Granny Smith apple)
2 tablespoons roasted
   peanuts, crushed
1–2 tablespoons ready-made
   crispy fried onions,
   to garnish

SAUCE
3 tablespoons palm sugar
3 tablespoons fish sauce
2 tablespoons tamarind
   concentrate
3–4 tablespoons lime juice

Thai pestles and mortars are super-sized for a reason: to fit lots of ingredients in, and to avoid the juices and fish sauce flying out during pounding! Although this *som tam* salad is made using a pestle and mortar, I've set the Wok Clock up here to show you in what order to add the ingredients and help you to squeeze as much flavour out of them as possible, while pounding and massaging the sauce into the spongier ingredients. If you don't have a big enough pestle and mortar, just pound the garlic and chillies together with the sauce, then pour it over the top of the remaining ingredients and give it all a good mix.

1. Blanch the green beans in a pan of boiling water for 2–3 minutes, then drain and cool under cold running water. Mix the sauce ingredients together in a bowl.

2. **Build Your Wok Clock:** Start at 12 o'clock with the garlic, followed by the chillies, dried shrimp, green beans, tomatoes, sauce, the aubergine, green papaya and lastly the roasted peanuts.

3. Add the ingredients one at a time to a large mortar, in the order of the Wok Clock, and pound for 30–60 seconds before the next addition. Mix it all together well with a spoon between ingredients. Serve the salad garnished with crispy fried onions.

PEANUTS

VEGETABLES & SHRIMP

PAPAYA

AUBERGINE

SAUCE

Lime Juice

Tamarind

Palm Sugar

Fish Sauce

SPICY SICHUAN POTATO SALAD

PREP: 10 MINS | COOK: 15 MINS | SERVES 2

2 large Maris Piper potatoes,
   peeled and sliced into
   3–4mm (1/8 inch) slices
1/2 teaspoon Sichuan
   peppercorns, ground
   to a powder
2 tablespoons vegetable oil
1/2 thumb-sized piece of
   ginger, peeled and cut
   into matchsticks
2 spring onions, finely sliced
1 large red chilli, finely sliced
3 tablespoons Lao Gan Ma chilli
   oil or Chiu Chow chilli oil
2 tablespoons Chinkiang
   vinegar or rice vinegar
1 1/2 tablespoons light soy sauce
1/2 teaspoon sugar

Steaming the potatoes rather than boiling them keeps their shape and maintains a bite. The Sichuan peppercorns and chilli oil add a punch to the dish, which goes well with some steamed rice and a sweeter or more mellow main dish such as steamed fish or braised pork.

1. Place the sliced potatoes in a large shallow heatproof bowl and steam for 12–15 minutes until tender (see page 20).

2. Toast the Sichuan peppercorns in a dry wok, swirling them around on a medium heat for 1–2 minutes until they start to pop and become fragrant. Transfer to a pestle and mortar or spice grinder and pound or grind to a powder, then transfer to a heatproof bowl. Heat the vegetable oil in your wok over a high heat. Once smoking hot, pour the oil over the Sichuan pepper powder. Mix the ground peppercorns and oil together in a mixing bowl with the remaining ingredients until well combined.

3. Once the potatoes are cooked through but still holding their shape, toss them through the mixing bowl of sauce, then serve.

GLOSSARY

UK	US
aubergine	eggplant
baby sweetcorn	baby corn
baking paper	parchment paper
birds' eye chilli	Thai chili pepper
blitz	process/blend
chestnut mushrooms	cremini mushrooms
chilli flakes	crushed red pepper flakes
coriander leaves/stalks	cilantro leaves/stems (but coriander seed)
cornflour	cornstarch
courgette	zucchini
fish fingers	fish sticks
fish sauce	Thai fish sauce
gherkins	pickles
grill/grill rack	broiler/broiling rack
hob	stove
jug	pitcher/liquid measuring cup
kitchen paper	paper towels
lamb neck	lamb shoulder
lemonade	lemon-flavored soda pop
Little Gem lettuce	substitute with romaine hearts
Maris Piper potatoes	Yukon Gold potatoes
minced (meat)	ground (meat)
moreish	something so delicious that it's hard to stop eating it
pak choi	bok choy
plain flour	all-purpose flour
prawns (tiger)	shrimp (jumbo)
rump steak	sirloin steak
Shaoxing rice wine	Chinese rice wine
sieve	strainer
single cream	light cream
sirloin steak	strip steak
soft brown sugar	light brown sugar
spring onions	scallion
starter	appetizer
stock	broth
sugarsnap	snow peas
sweetheart cabbage	a pointed green cabbage, also known as hispi cabbage
takeaway	takeout
tea towel	dish towel
Tenderstem broccoli	baby broccoli or Broccolini
tomato purée	tomato paste

INDEX

ACKNOWLEDGEMENTS

I do envy the types of people who have the time and dedication to read through a whole cookery book from front to back. It's an ongoing joke between my wife and I that, after four years, whilst running around after our boy, she still hasn't had the time to sit down and read my last book! Although, if you are the inquisitive type who likes to know what happens behind the scenes, then perhaps read the acknowledgements first and then sift through your cookbooks backwards for a chronological show of how something so intricate gets developed. Writing a cookery book is a collective, magnificent feat, which requires highly skilled people with all different mindsets to work together. My thanks here are a real appreciation of everyone's input to the book.

Richard Watts, my agent from Ever Forwards PR, who is more flamboyant than anyone I know, could easily have his own TV show and whose enthusiasm for our work runs through every joint, muscle and bone in his body.

Eleanor Maxfield, Pauline Bache and the Octopus/ Hamlyn team for pushing me to engage the right side of my writing brain once again. Kris Kirkham, whose friendship and pictures paint more than a thousand words. Eyder Rosso Rosso Gonçalves, the ultimate photography assistant. Rosie Reynolds, our food stylist who seems to be able to make even a messy plate of food look stunning and super moreish, and Morag Farquhar for her beautiful props styling.

Adrienne Katz Kennedy, my writing partner in crime who picks my biscuit crumbs and greasy thumbprints off the pages. Once again, we have been ships who pass in the night where chapter by chapter, I've handed over to Adrienne who then sense checks my midnight madness with a strong cup of coffee early the next morning. I could not have done this so smoothly without you.

Freya Deabill whose beautiful illustrations turn my scribbles and wacky wok ideas into reality. It's an honour to have worked with such a talented and creative friend for over a decade and a delight to see how even the illustrations have moved with the times, whilst always managing to keep the core values of School of Wok in mind. Freya lives and breathes our Learn – Laugh – Eat motto and if you ever need some awesome design work, check out her website www.thebrandnewstudio.com.

Alex and Emma at Smith & Gilmour have wonderfully brought the whole book together and kept me grinning throughout the cover shoot.

And of course my ever-growing team @SchoolofWok. The last year has been a whirlwind of emotions and change and when teams come and go, I liken it in my head to passing the Olympic torch. Shannon McAuliffe and Ruby Hazel who have led the team so graciously for the last three years, along with Natalia Jacques, my photoshoot sidekick from the old days, now handing over to the new powerhouse of teachers, Emma Chung, Ryan Yen, Michelle Chau and a brand-new set of chef friends to come. Our production team Clare Cassidy Sefati, Chris Jackson, Lee Skillet and Arthur Barker, who know how to make me laugh and keep me smiling throughout the videos even when my writer's block is at its height. Hannah Dryden Jones, Head of Marketing and Sales who's risen the ranks through seriously hard work and determination. Yolanda Ocon, our 'queen of everything', who is currently keeping us cooing with update photos of her wonderful baby Leo. Beverley Benn our most kind and patient head of customer services who holds us all together so seamlessly, like a quiet, diligent mouse. My business partners: Nev Leaning, who sent me a photo willing me on to put it into the book, but unfortunately his chaise longue couldn't quite fit on a double page spread; Max Rees (the grocery genius); and Ben Marson who finally managed to get together after a gruelling year and a half wait to devour two kilos worth of Ben's Spicy Fried Chicken (see page 146) in six and half minutes.

To all my family and friends for always eating my food so willingly. And finally, a big cheers to you all for a celebration of School of Wok's ten-year anniversary in London's Covent Garden!